ISBN-13: 978-1484883631
ISBN-10: 1484883632

DEDICATION

For my parents, who have always offered endless inspiration, support and encouragement, and to whom I am eternally grateful for bringing me up in a home stuffed full of books.

Introduction

"There's no such thing as writer's block." No doubt as a writer you will have heard that before, probably whilst sitting there facing the monumental task of writing the remaining 78,998 words of your novel, having so far managed merely to write your name. And even that's been redrafted to exclude your middle name.

Of course there's such a thing as writer's block, but what's perhaps not so clear is how this can be defined. Defining what we mean by writer's block is important, because it's only through this understanding that we can fully appreciate what the problem is and do something about it.

No matter how many hours you sit staring at a blank sheet of paper or screen waiting for inspiration to fall from the sky or the writer's block to fall out of your left ear it's unlikely that you'll make much progress.

The first thing to point out is that you are far from alone. If you have ever struggled to find the words to continue or even begin a story or book then you are in good company. Most of us at one time or another have found that our imaginations feel dried up and that we may never write another word again.

But this isn't a medical condition, at least not normally. It's important to remember that writing is a very creative process. Not every word will be unique, but the combination of those words certainly will be. You will be using words that have been used billions of times before, but in entirely new ways, expressing new ideas, imagining new worlds and creating new people to walk that other world.

It's a lot to ask, and far more involved than merely jabbing at the keys on a keyboard in the hope that given eternity you'll end up creating a masterpiece. Or the complete works of Shakespeare.

You may have experienced that wonderful sensation of writing busily on a new book or story, with words flowing so freely that you feel almost puppet-like, desperately trying to write them all down as quickly as possible before they are blown away like the dust of a morning dream. Yet later on in that same story you may be struggling to get anything down at all. You may find that even turning to another book or story results in nothing much happening. You may start to panic, worrying that you have run out of ideas.

Relax. You haven't. The human mind is considerably more inventive and creative than that, and there is no such thing as a writer's block that can't be unblocked. It's simply a case of understanding why the block has occurred, and working out how to unblock it so that you can move on.

In many cases the reason for the block is a physiological one. If you haven't slept well recently, or you haven't eaten for a while, perhaps the weather is stiflingly hot or you've been worried about a family member who is in hospital then your mind is hardly going to be firing on all cylinders, and you will simply not have the energy needed to focus on your writing. There's no doubt at all that writing demands concentration, and concentration demands energy. Without enough sleep, food and drink you cannot expect to perform as well as you would like.

But often the problem is down to the story itself. All too often exciting beginnings which seem full of promise whittle out, leaving you looking at a beautiful shell with absolutely nothing inside.

Sometimes the idea simply doesn't work, but that's not to say it can't be made to work with the introduction of a different angle, or another dimension.

Sometimes the story will seem to dry up, and the enthusiasm is lost, preventing the words from flowing. This can sometimes be caused by your characters. Good stories are more character driven than plot driven. Good characters make a story, and make the plot through their decisions and their interactions.

If you have been forcing characters to behave out of character, your characters are flat one dimensional cardboard cut outs, or they have been forced into certain behaviours purely to suit the plot then this could result in you reaching an impossible point where it just feels wrong but you don't know why.

Whatever the cause of your writer's block it is rarely going to be the same every time, and for this reason you simply can't rely on just one or two techniques to get you through it. You can try standing up, drinking a glass of water, walking around a bit and sitting back down. You never know, it might work. But it is unlikely, and even less likely to work again in future.

What you are holding now is a huge collection of 105 practical ways to beat your writer's block. But I need to explain how to use this resource in the most effective way.

What I would not suggest you try to do is to sit down and read it cover to cover. My intention for this book is for it to be a 'dip in' book. Feel free to randomly open it at any page whenever you feel you are struggling with your writing. Let the book open at any page, (or if you are reading this on a Kindle or similar e-reader then feel free to simply flick through the pages quickly until you feel the urge to stop, or your thumb starts to cramp) and read the summary tip at the top. If it sounds intriguing then read the longer description beneath and perhaps try it out.

Although the 105 tips are written in summary form at the top of each page these often don't fully explain how to get the most from the advice, and don't explain why the tip may work. The longer description for each tip goes into much more depth, explaining how to use the tip effectively, ways in which you can vary the tip to suit you better, and an explanation of why the tip is likely to work, and how it works.

Understanding the rationale behind this sort of advice is important. These aren't simply writing games or writing exercises. Each one has been carefully chosen for this book specifically for its effectiveness in helping to work through a writer's block.

Having said that though, not every tip in this book will work for you, and of those which do, not all of them will work every time. The reasons for experiencing a block while writing are many and varied, and applying the same method each time isn't likely to help. It's important to have some understanding as to the problem, and then pick a technique in this book which is designed to help you.

At one time or another I have tried all of these techniques, and can certainly vouch for them being of enormous help. Having worked as a full time writer and copywriter for many years I have often been faced with the task of writing a huge number of words every day, sometimes producing 8,000 words a day for long stretches at a time. Writer's block isn't just a pain, it can mean missing deadlines, losing clients and losing credibility.

It has been important for me to have a range of techniques and understanding to draw upon in order to freshen up my writing and freshen up my mind.

The mind of a writer is an extraordinary thing, capable of constructing entire worlds that are detailed enough to be fully believable, and to hold those worlds for weeks, months or even years at a time in clear detail. But the mind of a writer is also treacherous, because it is really two minds.

As a writer you have a creative mind that is artistic, imaginative and enthusiastic, but you also have an editing brain which is constantly being critical, analytical and pours doubt on every sentence you write.

Very often writer's block is caused by the editing brain dominating the creative one, and holding it back. Many of the techniques in this book focus on this idea, and provide ways in which you can settle the editing brain down so that you are free to let your creative brain run wild.

It's important to remember that when you are writing you will not be producing the final version of anything which anyone will see. You are producing the first draft, and it is unlikely that very much of the first draft will survive intact and untouched by the time it is ready to be released into the world.

The worry though from a writer's perspective can often be that the words written down will be the same ones by which you will eventually be judged. They are not. They are merely the scaffolding put in place for your eyes only, allowing you to then work on the book in a more productive and effective way afterwards.

I hope you find these tips useful, informative, helpful and enjoyable. Feel free to write notes on the pages, glue bits of paper to those pages you particularly find useful or bend the corners of pages you want to come back to. I won't mind. It's your book after all. This is a book to be used, not to simply sit on a shelf and be admired.

Remember, no matter what people might say, writer's block is real, but it's also not incurable. You are a writer, it's what you do. You can't forget how to write, and your imagination is not a limited resource that will one day run out of ideas.

Give yourself permission to enjoy the experience of writing, abandon the idea that a first draft is something by which you will ever be judged, and remember, writing for a living is far better than having a proper job!

Justin Arnold

July 2013

Tip #1

"Write out six questions an interviewer might ask one of your characters."

The Idea

The best stories are not event driven, or scene driven, or even necessarily plot driven. Characters and characterisation is often the hallmark of the best stories and writing. If your story isn't doing too well, and you feel as though you've reached an impasse then it may well be that it's not your scenery or plot which is the problem, but the depth of your characters.

This method of overcoming writer's block forces you to focus not just on one of your characters, but on what motivates them, what drives them, what concerns them, what worries them, how they are feeling, what they're thinking, what their views are on events, and even on other characters.

It is important to step away from being the writer interviewing your character, and think instead of the sorts of questions an impartial and objective interviewer might want to ask.

Write out the six questions before even beginning to consider the answers. Only when you have written out all six questions can you then begin to visualise your character answering them. What you will often find is that simply the act of answering these questions fleshes out your character much more.

It isn't just the answers which are important, because it's very much how your character approaches answering those questions.

Do they feel confident about saying the first thing which pops into their head, or are they constantly trying to present a persona which may not be truly how they are feeling inside?

Do they resent the questions, and if so, why?

Don't feel that you only can do this with your main character. Sometimes it is interesting to do this with a fairly minor character. You might find that suddenly they need to step forwards and take a more active role in the story. Or it could be that their view on the situation gives you an alternative way of considering how to take the story forwards.

Tip #2

"Write about how frustrating it is that you can't think of anything to write about."

The Idea

This is the sort of bizarre reverse psychology which can actually work. Often the biggest problem writers face is getting started. Once you have begun the process of putting ink on paper, or hitting the keys on your keyboard and seeing words appear on your screen the process of writing suddenly becomes much easier, and the perceived block is all but forgotten.

What you will often find is that by starting to write simply about the process of writing, or about how difficult you're finding it coming up with ideas to write about, suddenly ideas begin to occur to you.

What you may find happening is that after writing one or two sentences about your experiences with writer's block, one or two ideas pop into your head, and you may even find yourself writing about those ideas.

In fact it's not unknown to begin writing about how few ideas you have, briefly mentioning that one idea has actually just occurred to you, and then to begin writing about that idea. You may even find that after a few sentences you're writing your article or story even before you've realised it, and simply by deleting the first few sentences you have what it was you tried to write in the first place.

It is important to remember that your imagination is unlimited, and the well of your creativity is infinitely deep.

Writer's block does not occur when you have no imagination, no creativity and no source of inspiration. It occurs simply when there is some sort of perceived block between those ideas and your conscious mind that is then required to realise them.

By tricking your conscious mind into writing even when it feels as though there is nothing to write about, you can often end up producing some excellent writing before your conscious mind has even caught up with what's going on.

Tip #3

"Try playing some music in the background. Easy listening, jazz and classical are good, but it's a personal choice. Just keep it as background music, and don't play it too loudly."

The Idea

This idea works in three different ways. The first and most basic way in which playing music in the background works is simply by helping you to relax.

One of the causes of writer's block is over-anxiety. Stressing and worrying about the possible inability to write creatively is inevitably self fulfilling. Playing calm and relaxing music can help you to unwind and release some of the anxiety which may be holding you back.

The second way in which playing music can help is by drowning out other distracting sounds. You might not always be aware of it but there may well be sounds either in the house or outside which are inhibiting your ability to relax and focus solely on your writing.

Whether it be people talking outside, traffic, sirens, alarms or other noises, either consciously or subconsciously it is likely that they will be pulling your imagination away from your pen and paper, or away from your keyboard, wrenching you away from your imagined world whilst forcefully reminding you of the world immediately outside your window. By playing relaxing music you can help to keep the world outside at bay, focusing more on the writing you need to do.

The third way in which playing music can help you to overcome your writer's block is by helping you to immerse yourself in the mood of the scene.

Think of it a little like the soundtrack to the film adaptation of your story. By playing a type of music which fits the mood of your writing you can find yourself feeding on the artistic creativity of the musician, visualising your story more effectively.

It's worth keeping this tip in mind whenever you hear a piece of music you feel might help to reflect a certain mood or evoke a certain feeling. Make a note of the music, and if possible obtain a copy so that you build up a library of music which you can play whenever you need to feel a certain way, whether that be energetic, romantic, anxious, angry or happy.

Tip #4

"Skip ahead to a section of the story or article which comes later on, and begin writing that section before coming back to where you were stuck."

The Idea

It can be infuriating to find yourself stuck on a portion of your story where you feel you are unable to break through to the next section, yet all the while having a clear idea of what needs to happen or will happen later on.

Beating yourself up because you are unable to get through one section whilst excitedly looking forward to getting started on a section of your story which might come either immediately afterwards, or perhaps not even until near the end is not a productive or sensible way of working.

There is no rule which says that you have to start your story at chapter 1 and write sequentially all the way through until the last chapter. If you're feeling frustrated and unable to achieve very much then it may be useful to select a scene, event or conversation which may not be scheduled to occur for some time, and get started on this straightaway.

The process of writing a section from your story you haven't yet reached can be liberating. You are no longer limited by the words which have just preceded it, and can instead allow your imagination much more free range than before.

It may well be of course that as a result of writing sections of your story out of sequence you may need to make changes either to earlier portions of your story, or even to the later sections when you eventually catch up with yourself.

That is fine, and indeed healthy, since the editing process is likely to help tie those sections together more fluidly. Yet at the same time the quality of your writing is likely to have been improved since you are writing with more enthusiasm.

Tip #5

"Change your targets from time based ones to word count targets."

The Idea

Although this tip might not suit everybody, since not everybody has the flexibility of extra time, if you are able to switch your targets away from time based ones then it can help to alleviate some of the pressure which is probably resulting in your writer's block.

If you tend to have a target of spending half an hour writing then you may find that either consciously or subconsciously the pressure almost immediately increases right from the very start. If you only have 30 minutes then you inevitably feel that you must start writing immediately, and that you cannot waste any of the time.

Unfortunately creativity and imagination don't always work to such time limited targets. Rather than thinking about spending 30 minutes writing, try a target of 400 words. Of course, the number of words you choose as a target will be up to you, but often this can be more successful.

By having a manageable and achievable target which is based on the number of words, and not on the amount of time you will try to spend writing, you are much more likely to find that you make productive progress.

You may well still find that you are able to write for much of the time you have scheduled anyway, but you won't feel guilty about sitting back and just thinking about what you are going to write. It is important to remember that writing is not a process which sees you constantly adding words to the page.

The actual creation of words in written or printed form is only the very last step in the process of creating characters, plot and story.

Of course is also worth noting the fact that by having a daily word count target you can more accurately schedule how long it will take to complete your short story, or novel.

Tip #6

"Close your eyes and imagine your writer's block as a physical thing wedged in your head. Picture it coming loose, and rolling all the way down to your finger tips. Grip it in your hand and then throw it far away."

The Idea

Visualisation can be a very powerful tool, and most writers and creative people tend naturally to be good at it. When visualising the block, you can see it almost as a huge boulder, perhaps like the one from the Indiana Jones film.

Try to picture a tunnel inside your head with all your creative ideas leaping up and down, desperate to escape, but trapped behind the huge boulder. See the boulder starting to loosen and really immerse yourself in the scene.

Picture the boulder, smell it, hear it and as it finally comes loose see all your ideas cheering and running free after it. When the block reaches your finger tips, keep your eyes closed and literally throw it away.

Feel the creative ideas running down to your hands ready for you to start typing or writing away. It's important to take the time to let this visualisation technique work, and not to hurry it. The whole thing should take at least two or three minutes.

Taking the time to visualise this makes you stop focussing on the task in hand, the next chapter, scene or article, and instead gets you to focus on something completely different. But at the same time you end this visualisation process with a positive expectation that something creative will come.

Don't wait once the block has been thrown away, get those hands on the keyboard and expect the ideas to come. By expecting, and not just hoping, you stand a much better chance of actually getting something on paper.

Tip #7

"Try to write one single sentence which is as long as possible, say 300 words. You are not allowed to use conjunctions (and, because, but, or), but you can write about any topic, including writing about the exercise itself."

The Idea

Sometimes the secret to breaking through a writer's block is to actually increase the pressure and the restrictions. This tip is one example of how you can do just this.

No one would recommend writing sentences of up to 300 words, nor writing without the use of conjunctions. But the attempt to do so is likely to both distract you from your article or story, freeing up your subconscious to work through any particular problems you're currently facing, as well as getting you to put words on paper, thereby overcoming the fear of a blank white page.

Exactly how strict you are with enforcing such a role is of course entirely up to you. You are also free to adapt this tip, challenging yourself to write a sentence of perhaps 150 words, without using any word which contains a 'W'.

As a guide, the most common conjunctions which you may feel you would like to attempt to write a sentence without include 'and', 'but', 'or', 'yet', 'for', 'nor', 'so'.

For a greater challenge you might also consider excluding the following conjunctions: 'even though', 'if', 'after', 'wherever', 'until', 'when', 'while', 'although', 'as', 'provided that', 'as if', 'that', 'as much as', 'as though', 'because', 'though', 'as long as', 'before', 'in order that', 'in case', 'lest', 'once', 'by the time', 'even if', 'as soon as', 'only if', 'since', 'so that', 'than', 'till', 'unless', 'whenever', 'where'.

Tip #8

"Write the words, 'I can't think of anything to write about. The next bit of my book/story/article needs to be about/describe/explain...' and then keep going."

The Idea

This is another example of how it is possible to sometimes trick your own brain into overcoming writer's block. If you are stuck on a particular part of your story or article then what you will normally do is to let the ideas and the problem run around in circles in your head.

The problem is that the writer's block is also in your head, and this is what may be stopping you from making progress. The answer may well be to try this tip.

Let's say for example that you are stuck on a particular part of your story. By forgetting about writing the next paragraph or chapter of your story you fool your subconscious into thinking you are not actually writing your story for now.

By the time you have written the words 'I can't think of anything to write about. The next section of my story needs to describe...' you may well find that at least a rough idea of how your story is going to continue begins to form in your head. Perhaps that sentence continues by describing what happens next, allowing you to go into more and more detail until you are effectively writing the next section of your story before your subconscious mind has caught up with you and realised what you are doing.

If you don't feel that this is likely to work for you, don't dismiss it. Yes, it does sound a little bizarre that it is possible to consciously and deliberately fool yourself into writing.

But the truth is that it is very possible to trick your own mind into overcoming writer's block. The main reason for this is simply that writer's block is itself a trick of the mind, and nothing else.

Tip #9

"Drop a rubber or something on your keyboard to generate a few random letters. Now come up with a sentence in which each word begins with the next letter in the sequence."

The Idea

Of course there are various ways in which you can generate a few random letters, the easiest of which is perhaps to simply shut your eyes or look away from the keyboard and let your fingers come down at random. The idea is simply to generate a few letters, perhaps no more than half a dozen unless you're up for a real challenge.

The process of concentrating on words and writing without being encumbered by plot, character, scene or even deadlines can help to you overcome writer's block. Often it is the process of starting to write rather than the writing itself which is the problem.

This simple sort of exercise can be adapted in a number of ways. You could choose a word at random, or even the last word you wrote in your article or story, and use this as a sequence of letters.

So if the last word you wrote in your story was 'away' you would try to write a four letter sentence or phrase in which the first word begins with 'a', the second with 'w' and so on. Perhaps your sentence might be 'A watch arrived yesterday.'

You can also do a similar thing when out and about, using the string of usually three letters in a car's registration plate. If nothing else, this is an exercise which at least helps to pass the time on a long journey!

Tip #10

"Go back to an old place of work and remind yourself why you chose writing as a career."

The Idea

A great many writers only come to writing as an occupation after having pursued alternative career choices. Few people finish college, decide to be a writer, and then have the luxury of being able to indulge their love of writing from the word go.

Many writers initially feel thankful that they have been able to move away from the timetabled rigours of a 9-to-5 office job, working for a boss, attending meetings, enduring training days, staff appraisals and all the rest of the baggage which goes with trying to earn a living.

But sometimes when sitting in your own home, a mug of tea by your side, slippers and cat on your feet, the sound of birdsong drifting in through the open window through which you look out upon your garden, it is easy to feel frustrated and unable to make any worthwhile progress. The lot of a writer suddenly seems less appealing.

This is where it can be helpful, or at the very least reaffirming, to revisit somewhere you used to work in those days before an old biro was all you needed to put bread on the table. In some cases you might well be able to revisit an old workplace, and drop in on some former colleagues. In other cases just simply visiting the location is enough.

Try getting up at the crack of dawn, putting on a suit, sitting in a traffic jam during rush hour, and then ask yourself whether a little spell of writer's block might not be such a bad alternative after all.

Tip #11

"Write a postcard to one of your characters asking for help."

The Idea

All good stories are essentially character driven, and often the cause of writer's block can be attributed to a character related problem. Perhaps your character is not fully fleshed out yet, or perhaps your character has unwittingly behaved in a way which doesn't seem to fit either their previous behaviour or your imagined impression of them.

One of the fascinating experiences which writers often enjoy is when characters start to come alive, and begin to dictate what happens, or how the story unfolds, making the writer almost feel slightly redundant.

This is a great point to reach because it becomes easier to some extent to visualise how characters will react, interact and respond to certain situations and events.

This tip picks up on the importance of characterisation and understanding your characters, and your interpretation of who they are.

By writing a postcard or a short letter to one of your characters you flesh out your own concerns or queries regarding who they are, what they think of the current situation, why they have behaved the way they just have, or why you are surprised at their current responses or behaviour.

Simply posing the questions or making the observations will inevitably help you to visualise your character as a real person.

Allowing your character to break free from your notepad or your computer monitor can be both liberating and fascinating. If you normally type on a computer then you may try writing a postcard or note by hand.

You might even pop it in an envelope, and post it to your home address. This helps make the whole thing feel as though you really are writing to a real person, and the chances are that when your postcard arrives at your home address a couple of days later you end up reading it not as yourself, but as the character, having allowed your subconscious to mull over his or her possible responses to the question or observations made.

Tip #12

"Turn your screen off, or turn it away from you so that you can't see what you're writing."

The Idea

The biggest problem for most writers, especially those who use a computer, is that throughout the entire writing process you are constantly, editing, criticising and proofreading everything. Most word processing programs underline potentially misspelt words in red, and highlight grammatical inaccuracies and punctuation errors with green. This is decidedly unhelpful.

The best writing tends to be that which is written freely, unhindered by constant editing and criticising. The flow of writing becomes more consistent since the focus is more on the writing than on the spelling, punctuation, grammar and formatting. There is time for all that later on.

This tip therefore gives you the chance to focus on the writing rather than on the editing. Ideally you would type using a computer whilst looking either at the keyboard, out of the window, or a blank bit of wall.

But inevitably most people will find their eye drawn naturally to the screen. The moment you start to see that you have been writing all in capitals, or the computer has underlined half of your words in red you will find your creative flow stemmed quite quickly.

The fear of making a mistake is often one of the primary causes of writer's block, and so by switching the screen off, turning it away, or draping something over the screen so that you can't see your writing, you can focus more on the creative side of the process.

Of course there is a small danger with this tip. If you inadvertently switch focus to an alternative application from your word processing program then you may find that all of your typing is lost.

My recommendation is to switch to a word processing program which enables you to hear an auditory click every time you hit a key on your keyboard.

I use a free program called Q10 which you can download by visiting http://www.baara.com/q10. This means you can comfortably hide your screen whilst knowing that every letter is appearing in your document rather than simply switching the focus from one desktop icon to another.

Tip #13

"Try using voice recognition or dictation. Standing up and walking about can give you a different viewpoint and feeling."

The Idea

Your brain needs blood. Lots of it. But the problem is that if you sit down in a chair for ages your brain is really only getting a basic to mediocre supply of the red stuff.

By standing up and walking around you help to get the blood flowing a little quicker, your joints don't feel as stiff, and you may feel a little more active and energised than when sitting like a replica of Rodin's statue 'The Thinker' in a squashy chair.

Sometimes it can simply be the very act of standing up and walking away from the keyboard and monitor which can help break the cycle of staring blankly at a screen that's staring blankly back at you.

If you have a good quality microphone then you can either use voice recognition software to record your words and have them automatically transcribed for you, or you could simply record the sound file and then play that back afterwards, typing it up or writing it out yourself.

Of course if you have a dictaphone then you can sit, stand or walk about anywhere you like, either in the home, or even when you are out and about. If you have a long journey to do then having a dictaphone with you can be a great opportunity to get lots of writing done when normally you wouldn't be able to do any.

Sometimes simply being able to look away from the screen by using voice dictation software helps you to think more creatively because you are not assessing the accuracy of your writing at all.

Whether you are staring out of the window, or staring blankly into the middle distance, you're able to focus on the words, their meaning, their pace and their shape, rather than on their spelling, grammatical accuracy and the punctuation.

It is important to remember that voice dictation software is not 100% accurate, and it will require a little bit of training and some patience before the accuracy is sufficient.

However, for this to work you must resist looking at the words as they appear magically on the screen because you will be tempted to keep correcting any misheard words which appear.

Tip #14

"Disconnect the internet, pull your telephone cable out of the wall and switch your mobile off."

The Idea

The digital age is the writer's curse. Yes, computers have made some aspects of writing more convenient, and yes, online social media provides great marketing opportunities. I will even concede that the internet is a valuable source of inspiration, information and ideas.

But the internet, e-mail, telephone and mobile phone are all terrible distractions. The entire world and everything in it is but a click away, and if we haven't received an interesting message, e-mail, link, text or call in the last 10 minutes we start to panic and wonder whether the world has forgotten we exist.

Switching off from the world, or at least switching off from online and telephone distractions, can significantly improve the chance that you will be able to focus more consistently and more effectively on the writing task in hand.

Granted those distractions are still only moments away, but somehow making the positive decision to disconnect yourself from the world for half an hour, an hour or a morning can make more of a psychological difference than you might imagine.

Often the temptation whenever you reach the end of paragraph, or section of writing, is to quickly glance at your mobile phone, or quickly check to see if you've got a new e-mail. But this albeit very brief task is constantly distracting you from being fully involved with your writing.

Unless you are entirely absorbed in your writing, unimpeded by technological temptations, you will find even the mildest of challenges virtually insurmountable, throwing the towel in early and claiming writer's block before dashing to your social media platform of choice and bemoaning the problems that beset a writer.

Tip #15

"Write a set of instructional notes as though for someone else who will be writing the next section of your story, book or article."

The Idea

If you're feeling stuck with a certain part of your writing then imagine being able to leave a few notes next to your keyboard, get up, walk away and have somebody else do the writing for you.

Although this tip doesn't provide free access to your very own author substitute, it does help you to break free of the self-inflicted pressure which may be causing a temporary writer's block.

Simply by writing out notes in a format which could possibly be used by somebody else you will help to consolidate your thoughts and ideas in a more concrete format. The process of writing out these instructions and notes will help to pull together the various ideas which are probably swirling about somewhere at the back of your mind.

By writing out instructional notes, and then walking away from them, your subconscious will have something more concrete to work on, and you may very well find that when you return to resume your writing you will find the process a lot easier than it was before.

Your subconscious is an amazing resource, but unfortunately it is also one which can work against you. Almost certainly any issue relating to writer's block is in some way tied to the way your subconscious is feeling or reacting. But it isn't your enemy, it simply feels like it from time to time.

Your subconscious is also a very powerful tool, and able to process, sift, sort, realise and organise thoughts and ideas even when you are not consciously thinking about your writing.

This tip helps to provide your subconscious with something concrete and relatively structured to work on, which is why going through this process can help you to overcome writer's block fairly quickly.

Tip #16

"Read someone else's writing. Perhaps that book you never get round to. Just a few pages mind."

The Idea

Sometimes we can get so caught up with our own words that we become enmeshed in our own web. Sometimes the inspiration we need is to look outside of our own writing. Every writer has their own unique voice, their own style and their own approach.

Simply taking a little time out to read what somebody else has written, to hear another voice, discover a different style and a different approach is all that is necessary to help us feel renewed and ready to approach the challenge more positively.

What I am not suggesting here is that you try to change your own style and emulate the voice used by somebody else. But very often just listening to another voice helps us to rediscover our own.

Sometimes you'll want to simply pick up a familiar old book and dip in. But I would suggest that instead you pick up a book that you've never read.

We all have them sitting on our shelves, stacks of books which either we have been given, or we picked up in some sale or other, and which have been dusted that many times we've lost count. Yet we never actually sit down and read them.

By getting into a book like this you will be able to discover a completely different voice, and this in itself is refreshing after we have become so self obsessed with our own writing voice.

Of course the better quality the book the more likely it is to be inspiring. Poor quality writing may not be terribly inspiring, although you may feel so frustrated by it and so convinced that you could do better that you end up throwing the book to one side and proving it.

What I would advise against is thinking that reading almost anything other than your own writing is likely to be of benefit. Once you start reading blog posts online you are a dangerous click away from many hours' worth of distractions.

It is better to absorb yourself in several pages of a good book, well away from the temptations of a computer.

Tip #17

"Start writing on a blank page about your writer's block and why it's not going to beat you."

The Idea

One of the most daunting things to ever sit in front of a writer is a blank white sheet of paper, or a blank white screen. It is almost as though the whiteness is a challenge, or a threat. As though making one single mark on the paper is going to commit the writer to something permanent, unchanging and definitive.

Utter nonsense of course, but sometimes it can be that blankness which fools the writer's brain into matching that blankness. So the answer of course is to remove the blankness in front of the writer, and start to get the brain working with words again.

Words certainly aren't permanent, and whether it's a computer screen you're looking at or a pad of paper, those words can be deleted, torn out, screwed up and thrown away. So if you're finding it difficult to make progress with your own writing, use this tip and start writing about your writer's block.

But this isn't simply an exercise in removing the blankness from in front of you, defiling the crisp white sheet and sending writer's block fleeing in terror, it's very much about trying to create a positive attitude to writing.

By writing about why and how writer's block is not going to beat you, you are sending out positive encouragement to your subconscious.

As the page becomes less blank, as the words start to flow and your writer's brain begins to get back into gear, that positivity and enthusiasm is likely to make it easier for you to switch over at any point to the writing you intended to do.

Don't be afraid to simply leave the writing about writer's block unfinished and there on the page as you begin your intended writing in earnest. Handwritten text can be copied out, and text on the screen can be deleted. But if the page is no longer blank, often that's all it takes to banish the block.

Tip #18

"Imagine your writing as a maze. If you hit a dead end, back up to where you had a choice and try going in a different direction."

The Idea

The analogy of writing being like navigating through a maze is actually not far off the mark. Almost regardless of what it is we are writing about, inevitably we will be constantly making choices and decisions. Each choice we make necessarily opens up opportunities, whilst making alternatives more difficult or impossible.

Sometimes those choices will be very subtle and won't have too much significance, whilst at other times a seemingly simple and straightforward decision can have far-reaching ramifications. A character's reaction or response in one situation necessarily makes it harder to alter their behaviour later on without solid justification and cause.

If you have reached an impasse with your writing then it may very well be that any choice you made either fairly recently or quite possibly further back in your writing has resulted in you reaching what appears to be a dead end.

Rather than trying to smash your way through the brick wall in front of you, or sitting there staring at it in the hope that sheer willpower and patience will eventually cause the bricks to crumble, it may be more beneficial to back up a little to the last point in your writing where you made a choice.

Perhaps it was an event which occurred, a conversation between characters, or even a character's response in a given situation. Go back through your writing and identify a recent section in which you as the writer were given a clear choice between one or more ways forward. Consider what your alternative, or your alternatives, were at that stage.

By ignoring your subsequent writing, and continuing your story from that point, but following an alternative path, you could find that although your route is not the one you had originally planned, the journey might be easier, and the landscape more fresh, inspiring and promising than your original destination would have been.

Tip #19

"Write something completely absurd, such as having your main antagonist suddenly break out into song, or your protagonist steal a car."

The Idea

One of the ways in which it is sometimes possible to beat writer's block is to write something which you have absolutely no intention whatsoever of keeping. It is also sometimes quite liberating to write something utterly ridiculous and absurd, throwing aside the rules and the limitations which can end up fettering your creativity.

It is funny but sometimes you can sit in front of a pad of paper, or at a computer, and feel that you are completely unable to come up with even a single sentence.

Yet the moment you allow yourself to abandon your plot, to completely rewrite your characters and to go absolutely mad, you can often find your imagination becomes a little more colourful, your enthusiasm steps up to the mark, and the words begin to flow again.

Obviously the stuff you come up with will be utter rubbish, but knowing full well that you have no intention whatsoever of keeping those words in the story can often allow you to get over the hurdle which is currently holding you back.

It is perhaps important to imagine writer's block not so much as a brick wall in front of a cliff face which goes on for hundreds of miles and which is utterly insurmountable, but as a hurdle which may be a little daunting at first, but with the right technique and effort can be vaulted easily, after which you have a clear run ahead of you.

So perhaps what you might try doing is to introduce an element which is utterly bizarre, such as having a dragon suddenly descend in the middle of an otherwise fairly sensible urban tale.

Or perhaps your antagonist suddenly decides he's going to live as a woman called Gladys from now on, or maybe your protagonist decides that being a hero is too much hard work, and heads off to rob a bank.

The more absurd and ridiculous the better, and you'll probably find yourself enjoying this exercise, helping you to feel positive about the writing process again. You never know, you might even find yourself coming up with an idea for a completely new story!

Tip #20

"Try writing a sentence which does not include the letter 'e'."

The Idea

At first this might seem an almost impossible challenge, yet it is actually perfectly possible. This kind of word game challenge where sentences or paragraphs are written with one or more letters being deliberately avoided is called a lipogram.

A particularly intriguing and impressive example of a lipogram is the novel Gadsby by Ernest Vincent Wright, published in 1939. This book runs to 50,000 words in length, but remarkably does not contain a single example of the letter

E. Wright set himself the challenge of writing an entire book without the letter E, and whilst it may not be an award-winning example of literature, it does not sound in any way forced, and has been praised for its literary merit.

It is usually best to begin by thinking of any random sentence, and then trying to reword this so that the letter E is not included. It is important to remember that there are many commonly used words such as 'the' and 'her' which include the letter E, as well as certain plurals and past tenses.

By imposing this constraint you find that you are no longer able to be lazy in your choice of wording, instead focusing much more on using alternative vocabulary to express what you want to say. This is a different way of working, and challenges your creativity and your writing skills in a different way from normal.

Not only can this be a helpful exercise in overcoming writer's block, but it can be an amusing game that can be played at almost any time, anywhere.

Of course there is nothing to say that you can't simply continue your article, story or novel whilst carrying out this exercise at the same time. If you're finding it hard to motivate yourself to continue with your writing, actually constraining your writing in this way may bizarrely help free up your creativity and get you going again.

This exercise can also be adapted in a variety of ways. You might choose a completely different letter such as 'T' or 'A', or even a combination of letters to avoid.

Tip #21

"Write a diary entry for one of your characters, a shopping list, or a letter to a distant aunt."

The Idea

Sometimes the most mundane of descriptions or writing can help to break through a block. Since all good writing, at least fiction writing, is character driven, most problems tend to be character related.

Often the best way of overcoming a character related problem is to try a character related solution, and this technique helps to focus on a particular character in a way which is likely to be quite different from your normal writing.

Whether you choose your main character or a relatively minor character doesn't necessarily matter, but what is important is to think through their mind about something which may not necessarily be related in any way at all to the story or recent events.

In this way you are fleshing out your character beyond your story, and this is often the best way of creating realistic characters which behave in realistic and justified ways, helping to make it easier to drive your story forwards.

If you have found that your writing has ground to a halt, and you can identify one of your characters that seems to be problematic, then use them in this exercise.

By thinking about what sort of shopping list they might come up with you will inevitably be fleshing them out by thinking how they live, what sort of things they eat, what their home is like and so on.

If they're writing a letter to a distant aunt then there'll probably be talking about a whole variety of topics, including things that have happened recently in the story, but from their own unique perspective.

As a writer you will often find that you are looking at events from your perspective. This can be a problem, and can often result in your writing becoming either stale or stagnant.

By thinking about recent events through the eyes of one of your characters you may well find that inspiration finally dawns.

Tip #22

"Put the television on and tune in to a show you don't normally watch, and aren't familiar with, and then don't watch it. Close your eyes and just listen, and let your imagination paint the picture. Do this for just three minutes, then switch it off and let your mind slide back to your writing."

The Idea

Generally speaking writers have fantastic imaginations, but sometimes that doesn't feel the case. If your imagination has stopped working for a bit and you're finding it difficult to make progress with your writing then one technique that can be helpful is to stimulate your imagination in a different way.

Instead of staring at a blank sheet of paper or a blank computer screen trying to imagine words appearing in front of you, using the sound from a television show you're not used to can help your imagination to start working again and stimulate your creativity.

I recommend using the television rather than a radio simply because radio plays are designed to be delivered only using audio.

Television programmes are usually reliant upon visual clues and information, and if these are missing your imagination will need to work harder in order to fill in the gaps and create the scene as a visual image in your mind.

As long as you aren't familiar with the television show, the sets or the characters, you'll find your imagination uses the auditory clues to create what may well be a completely different scene to the one actually being broadcast.

Of course, this doesn't matter, and is actually a good thing, because the exercise is designed to stimulate your imagination and get the creative part of your brain freed up and achieving something.

By then switching back to your writing you may well find that your creativity has started to flow, and you are able to imagine your story, your characters and your settings more clearly and more visually in your head than before.

However, it goes without saying that this technique should not be overdone, since listening to the television for hours at a time will not help you to complete that novel on time!

Tip #23

"Stand up, walk away and start something like the washing up, and then compose only the first sentence out loud."

The Idea

Quite apart from getting you to walk away from the computer, stretch your legs and enjoy a change of scene, even if it is looking at your dirty dishes, there is a reason why this technique can sometimes make a big difference to the challenge of getting started with your writing.

Sometimes the hardest thing about writing is the writing itself. Not just the composing of ideas, or the phrasing of words into a sentence, but simply hitting the keys on the keyboard, or putting the pen nib to the paper.

By plunging your hands into hot soapy water and getting on with a mundane task such as washing up some pots, you deny yourself the ability to carry out the physical act of writing.

Knowing that you can't possibly do any writing right now with wet hands your subconscious no longer feels the need to hurl doubts and anxieties at you, which means that you may well find it easier to get your creative juices flowing once again.

Challenging yourself to come up with just the first sentence, and to do this out loud, you will find that not only do the words come a lot easier, but you will often find that the next sentence, and in fact the next section of your writing starts to become clearer in your head.

But avoid the temptation of trying to compose more than one sentence. If you do that then you will almost certainly forget the exact wording you came up with, and when it comes to sitting back down again and trying to write the words out, you may find yourself frustrated that you can't quite remember exactly what it was you came up with, negating any benefits of this technique.

If you have ever wondered why some of your best ideas occur to you whilst you are on the toilet or in the shower, this is the very reason, and the reason why this technique can be very effective. If nothing else, at least you'll have lovely clean dishes.

Tip #24

"Put the kettle on, then write a paragraph while you wait for it to boil. Then pop the teabag in, and write another."

The Idea

Sometimes one of the biggest problems when it comes to writing is sitting down and telling yourself that you have a whole half hour ahead of you, an hour, or even the entire morning to write. That should feel as though you have a good long stretch of time, but it can also feel like a sentence, and not the type with a full stop at the end.

This technique provides you with such a short space of time that it feels as though there is no pressure whatsoever.

By putting the kettle on you know you only have a few minutes until it boils, and so sitting down with a pad of paper, or your laptop, and just throwing out a few quick words before the kettle boils makes it feel as though you're not really writing at all, you're just occupying yourself whilst waiting for the kettle to finish boiling.

The same thing happens when you dump the teabag in the cup. You know you've only got a few minutes before your tea becomes too strong, and so again all you're doing is occupying yourself briefly while you wait for your tea to be ready.

What you will often find is that in the course of making a cup of tea you will have written at least a paragraph or two. But more than that, you will have started writing, demonstrating to yourself that you have beaten the block, you've added to your story or your article.

That psychological breaking through the barrier, even if only with a paragraph or two, can make a surprising difference. Once your cup of tea is made and is sitting on the desk next to you, you'll usually find it much easier to carry on writing having already made that initial progress.

Of course, if you don't drink tea then please feel free to adapt this, either for your mug of filter coffee or other beverage of choice. I wouldn't advise swapping making a hot drink for baking a chocolate cake every time you're stuck. You're unlikely to get much writing done, and after a few chapters you may find your chair beginning to creak!

Tip #25

"Stand up, look at yourself in the mirror and tell yourself that you are a writer, and that you can write just as easily as talk."

The Idea

Writing is not entirely dissimilar to talking. There is perhaps more opportunity for planning and for refinement when committing words to paper, but ultimately it is still simply communication through words.

If you were sitting with a friend who asked you to describe your story, or the next section of your story, you would probably not feel that you were unable to continue with the conversation, and unable to talk with your friend because of a 'conversation block'.

This technique involves two different strategies. The first is to face up to yourself in the mirror, and make a statement which affirms the fact that you are a writer. Whatever else you might be, mother, brother, taxi driver, cook, you are also a writer.

By saying this out loud to your reflection you are effectively addressing your subconscious, and throwing it a logical argument which says that writers by definition write, you by definition are a writer, therefore you can write.

But it also goes on to remind yourself that writing is simply the putting together of words into sentences in order to express or communicate an idea. You can do that using words out loud, or you can commit those words to the screen or to paper. By reminding yourself of how easy it would be to simply talk out loud to a friend, you can help yourself to see through the obstacles put in place by your subconscious.

If this technique alone doesn't have the desired effect you can take it one step further by using a dictaphone or other recording device, and then just sit and chat out loud either to yourself, to the cat or to an imaginary friend, mulling over the ideas in your story, discussing the way forwards and rehearsing a few ideas, phrases, sentences and conversations.

Not only does this help to remind you that words can be strung together verbally as well as through a pen or keyboard, but by discarding the anxiety caused by the feeling that the written word must be refined, exact and more correct than the casually spoken word you can find that you are able to break through the barrier and continue with your writing.

Tip #26

"Go somewhere similar to a location in your story (wood, library, church) and pretend you are a character in your story. Make a note of observations, thoughts, feelings, responses, suspicions. A dictaphone or notebook is ideal."

The Idea

It can be hard sitting in your own home, perhaps in your home office or study, trying to write about people or events taking place in an entirely different situation. For all their imaginations writers sometimes need that direct experience to help act as inspiration.

Clearly it's going to be a little difficult to try this technique if your story happens to take place on a small moon orbiting a planet a trillion light years away, or takes place three miles beneath the North Pole.

But if you are writing a scene which takes place in a wood, a church, a railway station or some other location which isn't too far-fetched then you may find it helpful to put your pen down, get out of the house, and immerse yourself in that type of environment.

Try to put yourself into the mind of one of the characters in your story. It doesn't necessarily have to be the main character, but it would help if it's one of the characters who will be within that kind of setting. Again, if they happen to be a psychopathic axe murderer you may find this slightly harder, but the more you put yourself into the mind of your character, and then put yourself within an environment similar to that being experienced by your character, the more it can help to bring alive the feelings and sensations which the character would be likely to experience themselves.

You can find yourself noticing things that you might not even have picked up on were you to be locked in your study at home confronted only by a computer keyboard and a big mug of coffee. Try to pick up on things that you hear, different smells, and small things that you might otherwise overlook.

Make a note of these either using a notepad or a dictaphone, and when you return to your writing you may well find that some of those experiences, reactions, thoughts or observations help to flesh out the character, bring greater realism to the scene, and help inspire you to continue with your writing.

Tip #27

"Unlock your creativity by coming up with a list of five completely insane concepts, such as air bags made from cactuses (to encourage safer driving), slow motion mirrors or inheritance tax (oh no, that last one's real)."

The Idea

Not only can this be quite an entertaining exercise, but you might even find yourself coming up with one or two ideas you might want to take to the Dragons' Den for consideration!

The one rule with this exercise is that there are no rules. Anything goes, and the more bizarre and extreme the better. In addition to the cactus airbags and slow motion mirrors mentioned above, here are another few ideas I came up with last time I tried this exercise:

- Elasticated toilet paper (ideal for households which include people of all sizes and shapes, and for making the last few sheets stretch that bit further).
- An I-don't-really-know-what-I'm-doing indicator for vehicles being driven by someone who thinks their turning may be coming up sometime soon, but isn't quite sure on which side.
- A text speak mobile phone tariff which charges you one pound every time you resort to using txt spk.

- A personal cloud generator for when you're working at home and want to be able to look out at horrible weather rather than feeling resentful at missing all the sunshine.
- A magnifying glass that makes things smaller, for when you really don't want to be bothered with the small print, or for arachnophobes who wish to go bug hunting.
- A triple stage amber light for traffic lights, in which the first amber light represents "Ah no you don't, stay right where you are," the second indicates "You really ought to hold on there," and the last means "Oh go on then, you might as well now."
- An artificial mole which burrows underneath your garden, creating a network of tunnels and depositing piles of dirt in random locations across your lawn in order to deter real moles.
- Non-flammable petrol, making garage forecourts safer, and enabling the use of mobile phones whilst filling up.
- Inverse sunglasses for cloudy days, with inbuilt lights at the top which make it look as though it's a bright and sunny day.
- A mobile phone with no phone facility, or text message facility, for people with no friends, but who want to be able to use a calculator on the move, as well as crosschecking the current time in three different time zones.

Tip #28

"Take a break, go for a brisk walk for five minutes, just round the block, and make sure you sit down to write immediately you get back."

The Idea

The human brain uses energy at a rate of about 20 watts, which works out at about one calorie every three and a half minutes. That might not sound a tremendous amount, but it works out at the best part of 500 calories a day.

Despite the brain only representing around 2% of your body weight, it uses between 20 and 30% of your body's total energy intake, consuming around 75% of blood sugar and about 20% of your oxygen intake.

But of course all this energy use requires blood, oxygen and the associated energy to actually get up to your brain. The fact that it's on the top storey of your body means that you need a good strong cardiovascular system to make sure your brain is working on top form.

Simply going for a brisk walk means that your oxygen intake will be increased, your heart rate elevated, and your brain will benefit for some time afterwards from an increased supply of blood and oxygen. This is undoubtedly an excellent way of helping to give your brain the best possible chance of helping you get that writing done.

The key here is to make sure that as soon as you have been for your brisk walk you sit down straightaway, perhaps not even pausing to take your shoes off, getting started with your writing immediately.

Think of your brain as being a little like an engine, working more efficiently and more effectively with a decent source of fuel. Powered by indoor air and caffeine it shouldn't be a surprise if it doesn't seem to get going properly.

Let it never be said that writers lead a sedentary lifestyle. In fact if you're in good health, you are active and you get a decent amount of fresh air and exercise each day you'll actually find it easier to sit still and concentrate on your writing when you need to.

Tip #29

"Begin your writing session by writing about what you aim to achieve in your writing session."

The Idea

Most writers would agree that the most likely time for writer's block to hit is the moment you sit in front of the computer with a blank document in front of you and the morning's writing and targets stretching ahead. The difficulty is not in the writing itself, but more usually simply getting started.

This tip overcomes this initial problem by making sure that you get some writing down on the page straightaway. Simply writing about what it is you hope to achieve during the writing session is not likely to instil any sense of anxiety, and so writer's block is unlikely.

Once you have managed to get words onto the page, and you are no longer looking at a rather daunting stretch of blank whiteness, it can often be easier to then get started with the writing you need to do.

But perhaps more than that, by committing to written words what it is you hope to achieve during your writing session you are more likely to be better focused on that writing.

Often writers have reasonable but somewhat abstract ideas in their head, and find it challenging getting started with the process of translating those thoughts and ideas to concrete words. By already committing to words a general overview of your intentions it becomes less daunting, freeing you to get on with the writing itself.

For some people this technique is best done the very minute you sit down to get on with your writing, moving on from this exercise to the real writing itself without any break.

For other people it is helpful to have an initial session during which you write about what it is you aim to achieve in your later writing session, after which you take a break, allowing your subconscious to mull over the more concrete plan you have come up with, improving your ability to produce your writing a little later. If you're not sure which would work best for you, try both methods, and see which you find to be the most successful.

Tip #30

"Up the pace briefly. Put the kettle on and see how many words you can write before it boils."

The Idea

I've often found that just as I am about to sit down and get on with some writing something pulls me back and insists that I absolutely positively must have a cup of tea on my desk if I am going to have any chance of writing something worthwhile. Sticking the kettle on gives me a few minutes to idly stand around, when I could be writing.

Sometimes having a time limit that's ludicrously small, and at the end of which there is a 'reward', can help the creative juices to start leaking a little.

So try this: put the kettle on, and then sit down straight away, knowing that you only have until the kettle has boiled, at which point you must stop writing. You are to write frantically for just those two minutes.

What you mustn't do while trying this is to proofread or edit your work. Don't worry about the quality - don't even look at the screen if you happen to be using a computer. Just focus on getting as many words down as you can in the time it takes for your kettle to boil.

You could even make this a sort of competition with yourself. Check how many words you write, and make a note of it somewhere. Then next time you make a cup of tea, see if you can beat that previous word count.

Of course, like many of the exercises in this book what this trick is designed to do is to simply kick start your creativity and help you overcome the immediate hurdle.

When I try this I often find that whereas my mind was virtually blank before, once the kettle is bubbling the ideas start flowing. In fact on many occasions I've entirely missed the fact that the kettle has boiled as I've become so engrossed with the writing process.

Tip #31

"Write a memo to one of your characters asking them for clarification about something."

The Idea

A basic fact of creative writing and storytelling is that stories - all good stories - are essentially character driven. Therefore if you're having a problem with your writing the chances are high that fundamentally it's characters which are holding you back.

Sometimes this can be because in an effort to force your story to adhere rigidly to your preconceived plot, one or more of your characters are behaving in a way which doesn't fit the character which has so far been revealed.

Holding a character back, or forcing them to do something that doesn't fit comfortably with their behaviour up to that point can cause real issues. Having characters which are too flat can make writing dull and lifeless, sapping any enthusiasm from the writer.

So this tip is not only an effort to get the writer writing again, but also helps to address the potential problem, even if the writer is not consciously aware of what the problem really is.

Begin by choosing one of the characters from your story. It doesn't necessarily have to be the main character - it can be a fairly minor character if you like. Write a brief memo - perhaps even an email (sent to yourself) in which you ask them a few basic questions.

These questions could be along the lines of 'how do you feel about...' or 'why didn't you...'.

As you formulate the questions you will find three things happen.

Firstly your character leaps out of the pages of your book and becomes a real person, someone you can actually email.

Secondly, you start to think about the character, their role and behaviour in new and challenging ways as you think of the questions or problems you want resolving.

Thirdly, your writer's subconscious will immediately start working away in the background trying to answer those questions. You'll probably find that the answers pop into your head when you least expect it.

Tip #32

"Pick someone well known, and imagine them in your mind dictating to you. Write down the words you hear in their voice."

The Idea

This seems a bizarre idea, but it's one I use a lot. In fact it's one of my most frequently used techniques for getting started, or restarted, with writing.

Admittedly this works better if you're writing articles for marketing, web content or blog posts, because when it comes to writing short stories and novels it's always best to have the author's distinctive voice reaching the 'ears' of the reader.

But even so, I think that this can work as a way of kick starting the first draft at least, after which the author's own style can be woven into the writing if certain passages don't seem to fit.

What I do quite a lot if I'm stuck for ideas and my fingers seem to be magnetically repelled by the keyboard is to picture someone in my mind whose voice I can easily hear even if the word are mine. This might be a journalist or news reporter, it could be a chat show host, an actor, or even a fictional character from TV or film.

I then picture them in my mind talking about whatever subject it is I need to write about. Bizarrely I often find that this is extremely effective, and I have often written entire business articles simply by 'listening' to the person's voice in my head talking to me about the subject.

Of course, this tip could simply be an admission that I hear voices in my head, but then that probably is true for every writer anyway. We're all doomed to psychiatric examination at some point.

It doesn't even matter if the person you're picturing has nothing whatsoever to do with the subject you're focussing on.

I have written entire articles on the subject of fibreglass roofing by hearing the voice of Jeremy Clarkson in my head, and articles about mortgages and savings by listening to an internal monologue in the voice of David Attenborough. If it works, use it!

Tip #33

"Re-write the last paragraph in a different person, switching from 1st person to 3rd person or vice versa."

The Idea

The advantage of this tip is that you don't need to think of any new content at all, because the text you'll be using is already on the page. You don't even have to worry yourself about editing it, critiquing it or evaluating it.

This is simply a grammatical exercise, but one which is not only reasonably straightforward, but which can help you to think about the story from a slightly new perspective. This new perspective can often result in kick-starting the creative writing process.

For example, moving from one tense to another, or from one person to another, can help present the story in a completely different way.

By viewing the story as though the actions were happening in the past, rather than in the present, or by telling it in the first person as though it happened to you rather than to someone else, you can start to fill in the gaps which have been preventing you from making progress.

Sometimes re-writing the last paragraph in the future tense can help you to consider alternative possibilities or options, and writing from the point of view of a completely unmentioned character who may be only passively observing the scene can help you as a writer to step back from the writing and consider it more objectively.

Although this technique is essentially grammatical the real benefit of it comes through allowing you to view your existing writing through new eyes. What you may find is that once you reach the end of the paragraph this new writing perspective, style or point of view allows you to keep going.

Of course, if you do keep going, just keep going, but don't worry about accuracy, spelling, punctuation or grammar. You'll need to re-write it anyway to fit the style or person of the rest of the story, but at least you'll have something to edit.

Tip #34

"Keep a notebook with you at all times, and jot ideas down whenever they occur to you. Refer to this when writing, or when stuck."

The Idea

Many people would suggest quite quickly that if you don't cart a notebook around with you everywhere, or at the very least have a healthy collection of old napkins, torn bits of paper and envelopes with various scribbles over them, you can't really call yourself a writer.

But if you are facing writer's block it may be helpful to ask yourself two questions: how religiously do you really make a note of ideas, thoughts and phrases which hit you out of the blue, and how often do you refer to those notes at times when inspiration seems to have taken a back seat and left your text cursor flashing at you like a digital form of Chinese water torture?

It may not always be convenient to carry a chunky notebook with you everywhere, but don't let this mean that you're without the ability to make notes wherever and whenever an idea sneaks into your mind when you aren't looking.

Because those pesky little ideas will just as easily sneak out again, however brilliant they may have been and however much you may have been convinced you'd remember them.

If carrying a large notebook around with you isn't convenient then consider getting a very small notebook, like one of those shopping list notebooks, or even tear off a couple of pages and shove them in your pocket.

If even this seems like too much bother then perhaps your mobile phone has a notes application or option which you could use, and if you don't have time or the opportunity to write or type your thoughts out, perhaps dictating them is the answer? Many mobile phones today now have a memo recording facility, or you could use a dedicated dictaphone for when you're driving, for example.

But as well as making notes, it's all too easy to ignore them, while still complaining about writer's block.

If inspiration is lacking, pull out that notebook, look over your scribbles and listen to your recordings - you may just discover that you had the perfect answer months ago while shopping for Brussels sprouts.

Tip #35

"Write a review of a book or product you recently purchased online, such as through Amazon."

The Idea

Like most writers you have almost certainly purchased the odd book at some point, and there's a reasonable likelihood that an online retailer such as Amazon was involved, especially if it was an e-book you bought.

One of the huge benefits of buying books and other items online is that you can read reviews of them, written by other customers. These reviews can be very informative, very helpful, and sometimes very entertaining.

So if you're stuck with your writing, why not start your writing session by writing a review of one of those books or household items you've bought online recently?

Websites such as Amazon have a very easy to use review system, and you can generally leave reviews of almost anything you've ever bought from them.

The great thing about this writer's block technique is that you'll find it much easier to get started because it's only a fairly short bit of writing, and it's about how you felt in response to the book or item you received. This gives you something concrete to write about, and it's okay to write exactly how you feel - in other words, you can't be wrong.

But more than this, your review will provide a useful resource for other customers, and what you'll often find is that your review becomes rated, and sometimes receives responses. So your writing is not only helping to get your creative juices flowing again, you're producing something of actual value.

If you want to broaden your reviews to include books or products you haven't bought through Amazon then you could always start a blog, creating categories for each of the product types or book genres, writing your reviews as posts

Just as long as this doesn't end up taking up so much of your time that you no longer have time to do the writing you meant to do in the first place!

Tip #36

"Do something, or go somewhere, that is fresh and different to help boost inspiration."

The Idea

As a writer it can be easy to end up staring at the same four walls, the same screen and the same pot of pens for hours every day, and this isn't going to offer much in the way of inspiration.

Writing is about telling stories which involve people and places beyond the confines of your study or writing area. So it stands to reason that the most obvious way of breaking free from writer's block is to get out there and get inspired.

Make sure you take your notebook or dictaphone with you, and go somewhere new and different, or somewhere familiar but at an unfamiliar time. And just watch, and listen.

Take it in, absorb everything around you, step back and take in the big picture, then home in on one tiny and easily missed detail. Listen to what people are saying, how they're saying it, and what they probably mean.

If you are writing using a fountain pen then after a while your cartridge will run out of ink. Sitting there scratching away isn't going to achieve anything more than tearing the paper and making you more and more frustrated. Instead, the solution is simply to pop in a new cartridge.

Escaping the confines of your usual writing area is much the same as filling up your pen with fresh ink. The great thing is, it doesn't have to cost anything, and you can do it as often as you like.

Have a think about where you could go that is unfamiliar to you. Perhaps a park you've never been to, a museum or gallery you've never visited, perhaps a new exhibition or even a shopping mall.

Head off to a beauty spot, or a derelict housing estate, it doesn't really matter - when you start looking, and you realise you're there only as a writer, only to observe, you find that inspiration quickly starts to fill you back up.

I often take either a notebook, laptop or tablet with me and start writing there and then. Having a writing area or study at home is great, but just sometimes it can be a boon to escape from it.

Tip #37

"Always finish part way through a sentence before ending your writing session."

The Idea

One of the worst ways of finishing your writing session is to come to the end of the section you had clearly outlined or drafted in your head. Once you reach the end of a section, or a passage of writing you had in your head you reach more than a full stop - it can often be a brick wall.

Something which can be mildly infuriating is running out of time to write when you still have lots of ideas in your head and a clear idea of where you're going with your writing. It might be frustrating, but what you often find is that you are itching to get back to your writing, and to sit down and finish the ideas you had in your head.

So this idea takes this concept and forces you to finish your writing at a point where you still have a clear idea of where you are going next.

You don't necessarily have to finish halfway through a sentence, it might be halfway through a conversation, or halfway through a particular action or event. As long as you finish your writing session part way through an idea you'll find that you'll be anxious to try to get back to your writing, to carry on with it, and to finish the section you were on.

Once you get back into your writing you'll usually find that your brain slips easily into the world you've created, and the ideas begin to flow again.

If your previous writing session ended at what felt like a brick wall then all you'll be doing the next time you sit down to write is staring at that brick wall with no clear idea of where to go next.

But if you are able to finish one writing session part way through a sentence, an idea or a conversation, and you already know how things will develop from that point, then when you come to restart your writing you'll be able to get cracking straight away. Once that happens you'll then be more likely to keep going.

Tip #38

"Try writing at a completely different time to usual, such as before you have breakfast, right after lunch or last thing at night - even 3am!"

The Idea

I dislike mornings, and hate alarm clocks. Yet bizarrely my best time for writing is very early in the morning. I know that if I get up at 4am, and work straight through to around 9am I will get about twice as much done as if I start work at 9am and finish at about 5pm.

There's something peculiarly delicious about having breakfast and watching people heading off to work and school knowing I've finished my day's work. The only problem I have is getting up that early!

Most writers have a good time and a bad time during the day for working. For some people very early in the morning is best, whilst for others late at night is when the brain is firing its creative cylinders.

If you're finding writing a struggle then it's perfectly possible that you are trying to force your creative mind to work at a time that's really not suitable. If at all possible try changing the time when you do your writing and see if this offers any more success.

You may need to forgo that extra glass of wine and late night shopping channel marathon, head to bed an hour earlier and get up an hour earlier. It might not work, but it's a good idea to give it a try.

Of course, it is possible that the time of day when your brain is working at its best is entirely impractical. I know my brain's worst time for writing is between 9am and 5pm, which means that a normal office job was never going to be my calling.

Try doing some writing early in the morning, or during your lunch break, right before the school run, while the kids are doing their homework, or in the evening when it's quiet - basically, any time that's not your usual time for writing.

If you find it works, then the next challenge is working out how to optimise your day to best take advantage of your brain's preferred time for creativity.

Tip #39

"Randomly select a word from the dictionary. Now write a scene in which one of your characters receives a letter in the post which includes just that one word."

The Idea

As I mentioned in a previous tip (which you may not have read yet if you're one of those people who dips in at random) almost every single good story is essentially character driven, and if you're struggling with the plot you will often find that deep down it's the characters which are holding you back.

This tip provides two opportunities in addition to helping you get into the swing of writing again. By randomly selecting a word from the dictionary (your first choice, not your eighth!) you will be forced to take your writing in a different direction. This will allow you to relax, and to feel unconstrained by plot, pre-conceived ideas or good intentions.

It will also allow you to focus a little more on aspects of your character which you may not really have thought about before. Pick a character either at random, or one you feel is a little flat, a little forced or causing you some difficulty, and see how they would react to a note dropped through their letterbox with a rather odd word on it.

You can imagine the note to either be a handwritten one, or perhaps one of those ransom style notes where the letters have been cut out of a newspaper. It's entirely up to you, but be honest with yourself, and choose a genuine word at random.

If a very serious, perhaps somewhat flat character in your story suddenly receives a handwritten note through their letterbox with the word 'toadstool' on it, how would they react? What about if a fairly carefree character received a ransom style note with the word 'midnight' on it?

You may find that the resulting text doesn't have any place in your story, but it will help you think about your character more, and this may well help to move your story forwards. You never know, the concept you come up with could form the basis of an entirely different story altogether!

Tip #40

"Imagine that someone has just popped into the room to ask you what your next 500 words will be about. Summarise it out loud."

The Idea

Maybe it's the dog, or your child, your long suffering partner, or your editor - whoever it is you imagine walking in on you, stifle the urge to tell them to mind their own business and get the heck out of your study, and try instead to tell them briefly and simply what's about to happen.

Sometimes vocalising your intentions or immediate plans helps to not only solidify them, making them seem more real, more concrete and more achievable, but it can also help us to negotiate tricky situations or capture vague wisps of ephemeral creativity and tie them down.

That's half the problem with us writers. We have a vague notion of where we're going, but it's often caught up in feelings, vague images and impressions - not words.

We are interpreters of imagination, and that can be very hard sometimes. We have a vague idea of the next section, but when you're sitting in silence and you feel you have to pull those vague ideas into sharp reality through the bold use of black ink on white paper, it can seem impossible.

But by talking out loud you are avoiding that concrete black and white finality, because you're still playing with ideas, still looking off into the middle distance and imagining. It's easier sometimes to talk out loud about ideas than it is to commit them straight to printed or written words.

By summarising just the next 500 words, the next page, the rest of the chapter or the rest of the conversation you can help clarify ideas in a way which makes them much easier to pull just one step further, onto the page itself.

But by talking to someone else, either real or imaginary, animal, mineral or vegetable, you are forced to explain your ideas in a way which allows them to stand apart from the passage that's just been written. In other words you will need to put the next section into some sort of meaningful context, and this is what makes this tip so effective.

Tip #41

"Hide the Task Bar on your computer desktop, and remove or turn away all clocks and watches. Time doesn't apply to you anymore."

The Idea

Isn't it astonishing that with all the time saving gadgets and appliances we have today, saving us countless hours of work, we clock watch more than ever before? Clock watching and time awareness is one of the biggest causes of writer's block.

If you know you have an hour for writing then there's every chance that you'll quickly glance at the clock or your watch. It's never very reassuring, because your subconscious mind will simply calculate how much time you have left, and crank up the pressure. The more pressure you're under to write something creative, the less likely it is to be possible.

Of course, I fully appreciate that not everyone has the luxury of being able to ignore time for a while, but as a single father who has two school runs a day, various clubs and activities to provide a taxi service for, two large huskies requiring 8-10 miles a day and a full time job as a copywriter, I can still usually find an opportunity to switch off time for a while.

I usually find that if I get ahead of my usual work and block out a morning I can ignore the clocks, hide them, or remove them from the room completely, and then keep working until such time as my stomach tells me it must be about lunchtime. Alternatively I may go to bed early, rise at around 3am, and work through until my stomach tells me it is time for breakfast.

I find my stomach is a pretty accurate alarm clock, and certainly one that's less immediately frantic than a normal alarm clock.

The principle here is to remove the pressure of time, or at least to stop yourself from being consciously aware of it. The more consciously aware you are of exterior issues such as the exact time, and time you have left, the less your subconscious will be able to explore your imagination and provide you with a fluid stream of ideas and words.

If you really don't feel that this is ever possible for you to achieve, perhaps a writer's retreat is in order?

Tip #42

"Put your shoes on to write. Being in comfy slippers disguises the fact that you are actually at work."

The Idea

If you work as a bricklayer, schoolteacher or judge people tend to look at you strangely if you turn up for work in your comfy slippers, but as a writer your slippers are very often a part of your daily work uniform.

This can sometimes help to increase our comfort to the point where it doesn't really feel as though we're at work at all, and that's not helpful when it comes to getting our brains into work mode.

Some writers only ever write when wearing shoes, and some won't wear anything but a formal pair of work shoes. The difference in the way you feel can be quite dramatic, and just the act of putting a smart pair of work shoes on to sit down and write can help to put you into a better frame of mind for writing.

When going out to work most people go through a sort of ritual, smartening themselves up, ironing a clean shirt, putting on a suit, shining their shoes and putting them on.

This ritual can in part help prepare us for the job in hand. But as a writer there is no need to wear any particular outfit. You can wear your pyjamas should you so choose... or indeed nothing at all if that's what tickles your fancy.

But if you are finding yourself staring at a blank page with the words trapped behind an impenetrable barrier you may find that by wearing a 'writer's uniform', such as a tie, a smart pair of shoes or other more formal attire normally reserved for 'proper' jobs, interviews or meetings, the words come a little easier.

This separation of work from home is vital, and often writers struggle to achieve this. If your writing room or study is the back bedroom, or worse, a corner of the living room, then you are going to find it very hard to distinguish home and family from your job or role as a writer.

But to be successful you must address this, and dressing for work, even if just wearing a smart pair of shoes rather than your slippers, could help you step from home to work more effectively.

Tip #43

"Have a lit candle next to you. The flickering light can help to kindle creativity."

The Idea

Sometimes I think I was born into the wrong age. I use computers every day for my writing - I have a desk which includes a computer, a laptop, an iPad and an iPhone, all of which have a role to play in the process of delivering 6-8,000 words a day.

But given a free choice I would much rather spend my day on the opposite side of my study, where I have an old antique bureau stuffed with parchment style paper, quills, dip pens, sealing wax and candles.

There's something much more organic, more tactile and more alive somehow at that end of the room. Computers are so cold, so clinical, so precise and so dead.

Bringing something alive, something moving, something organic and natural into the immediate writing environment can help to foster creativity and 'set fire' to the imagination. It definitely works for me, and I know other writers who entirely agree, so it's something I fully recommend you try.

Whilst the flickering movement of a candle can have a real impact on how a writer feels, the same effect can sometimes be achieved simply by introducing something living or natural into the immediate vicinity. So you might try having a plant pot next to your computer, or a vase of flowers. As long as it isn't silicon, electrical or plastic you're likely to find that it offers at least some help.

For generations humans have stared into the flickering fire and told stories. There's got to be something in it! Staring into the flickering flame can become somewhat hypnotic, visually obscuring our vision from the distractions all around us, and helping to transport our imaginations into other worlds, other places, other times.

Obviously it goes without saying that having a lit candle burn down your study, or the water from a pot plant short circuiting your computer isn't going to help much. But done safely I am convinced that the introduction of these elements can make a remarkable difference. Put your preconceptions to one side and give it a try!

Tip #44

"Tell yourself out loud that in five minutes you will sit down and write 500 words. Five minutes later sit down, fully expecting to write 500 words."

The Idea

I recall being given a piece of advice when I first started teaching, and that was to always make sure that when instructing a class or group of children to do something, make sure to speak in a way which implies you have no doubt it will be done, rather than merely asking for it to be done.

Giving the impression that you have no doubts about your expectations creates a much more powerful instruction, and usually gets the job done.

This tip takes this same idea, and applies it to yourself. By vocalising your instruction in such a way that it becomes an expectation your subconscious mind will accept that instruction as though given by a third party.

It will prepare you for work, and when you sit down your subconscious mind will have already cleared away the clutter left by your conscious mind, leaving you free to sit down and get on with the real task in hand.

The more you expect to have success, the more success you will have. Similarly if you expect to fail then you're halfway to succeeding - in failing.

If you worry about having writer's block then you're fairly likely to develop writer's block, whereas if you expect to be able to sit down and get five hundred words down on the paper then you're much more likely to achieve this.

You might start small, since you're more likely to believe your spoken-out-loud instructions to yourself if you have already demonstrated that they work.

So you might tell yourself that in two minutes' time you will sit down and write one hundred words. Next time you can increase it to two hundred and so on, until you can instruct yourself with complete confidence that your subconscious mind will provide you with a clear path to success when the time comes.

Tip #45

"Choose a fairy tale, and write a paragraph which could be added to the end showing what happened next."

The Idea

The problem with fairy tales is that they all seem to finish with '..and they all lived happily ever after.' Life just isn't like that. It's almost certain that there is at least one person still alive within the fairy tale world who isn't happy about things. And it's also highly likely that something will turn up to make life just a little less rosy.

This idea takes a fairy tale from the point at which it traditionally ends, and asks you to continue it. It can be surprising just how easily the ideas start to flow, because you already have a created world and a cast of characters, all of whom come complete with a back story.

Once again, good stories are character driven, not plot driven, and with a set of characters all ready and waiting for you to play with, you're already being given a head start.

The fact that you are taking these characters from a fairy tale means that you've almost certainly been familiar with them all and their back story since you were a child. Coming up with the next part of the story isn't too hard.

Two things come out of this, apart from it being quite fun. The first thing is that you'll find yourself writing, which is always a good start.

I recommend doing this exercise, and then when you're done, carry straight on with your normal writing without changing to a new page, sheet or document. Just keep going. You can edit it later.

The second thing that may happen is that you find a new story idea developing. Whether it is based on the original characters, or you feel you can take a new direction with characters which are changed beyond their original moulds is up to you.

Tip #46

"Open a window, stretch, and breathe deeply for a minute. Then go straight back to your keyword or pen and paper and write."

The Idea

It's easy to forget, but writing is a physical exercise. Although you're not going to drop a dress size or be able to sprint a marathon just by tapping keys and clicking your mouse occasionally, your brain does use up energy simply by thinking.

If you sit in an office or study for ages at a time then it's perfectly possible that you're not getting a regular supply of fresh air. Your brain needs fresh air to operate properly.

Sometimes writer's block is simply your brain becoming sluggish because you're not feeding it enough oxygen!

But just sticking your head out of a window and filling your lungs up isn't enough. To get all that lovely fresh oxygen to your brain your blood needs to be shifting around nicely, and standing up and walking about can help get the blood flowing well. It really doesn't help your brain if all your blood is sitting in your feet! (Biologists and medical professionals, please understand I'm jesting here - don't write in to explain that just because I'm sitting down my heart doesn't stop. I realise this. But just sitting down all day can mean that your heart doesn't end up being in your work, which is just as bad.)

In all seriousness, it is important for all sorts of reasons to get up occasionally, walk about and get some fresh air. Even if it's just to walk downstairs, put the kettle on and then wander about the garden pulling up a few weeds while the kettle boils.

It's surprising the good it can do you, and as well as helping to freshen up your brain, and energise you ready for another round of paragraph pushing, it can also help alleviate the risk of blood clots, back problems, neck problems, eyesight strain, headaches and many other ailments.

Who knew that writing could be a such a dangerous occupation? Don't let this tip be an excuse to wander away from your writing to clean the toilet, wash the car, weed the garden, do the week's shopping, go swimming and have a coffee with a friend. Time yourself just five minutes per hour, or fifteen minutes every two hours.

Tip #47

"Change the colour of the document background to dark grey and have the text coloured light grey, so that you can just tell that your text is there, but you don't start to edit what you have written as you write it."

The Idea

Writers have two brains. The first is the one that's terribly creative, loves writing and is pretty good at it. The second brain is the editor, constantly second guessing the writer brain, criticising, judging, pointing out errors and sowing the seeds of doubt. As far as which brain is the one guilty for writer's block, it isn't hard to choose.

This tip effectively removes the second brain from the equation. Don't get me wrong, it is vitally important to have a good editor brain, but only at the right time.

Just as you wouldn't combine an apple pie and custard with a chicken casserole all on the same plate, it's not good to have your writer's brain and your editor's brain actively involved in the creation of your first draft at the same time.

If you use a wordprocessor to do your writing then it's a fairly likely bet that you spend a good deal of time looking at the screen. Even those writers (like me) who still need to stare down at the keys on their keyboard glance up every few seconds to see what's going on.

The problem is that with most wordprocessor any spelling mistakes are highlighted by a rather obvious wiggly red line, with potential grammar errors highlighted by a green wavy line.

Even without these features though, both of which can be turned off, the critical writer will tend to re-read the last few words, or the last sentence.

To make sure that this tip works properly it is important to switch off the spell checking and grammar checking features while you work. This is probably a good thing to do anyway!

Tip #48

"Leave a note on the page when you finish your writing session to prompt you when you return."

The Idea

Very often when you stop writing you'll have a reasonably good idea of where your writing will go next. The moment you stop writing, because perhaps you've run out of time, the kids need picking up or your stomach demands food, your creative mind will be sloshing about with ideas, possible phrases and next sentences.

By spending just a moment writing these down, rather like sticking a post it note to your work, you'll stand more of a chance of picking up where you left off when you return to your work.

The great thing about this tip is that if you get in the habit of doing it regularly you will start to find that your creative mind plans ahead for the little note you'll be leaving, and you'll find it easier and easier to jot a few ideas, phrases and prompts down in advance of your next writing session.

One of the most common causes of writer's block isn't a lack of ideas or creativity, but a sort of frozen state of fear at the threatening blankness of page before you.

By having a little note with prompts, ideas and phrases, possibly from yesterday or even last week, you'll have a starting point, ideas to think about, phrases to pick up on, and this makes it very much easier to get started again, and to get back in the flow of your writing.

If you're writing longhand using a real pen and paper you might almost use a sticky note, attaching it to the bottom of your work, but if you're using a computer then you may find that the word processing package you're using allows you to insert a shape, and colour it yellow, and then add text.

For example, if you're using Microsoft Word you can insert a shape by holding down the 'Alt' key and pressing the letters 'n-s-h' in turn.

Tip #49

"Use a simple text editor such as Notepad rather than a complex word processing package which offers spell checking and formatting features."

The Idea

The problem with most word processing packages today is that they offer far too many options. They're not really word processing packages any more - they're desktop publishing packages, and that's not really what a writer or author needs, at least not to begin with.

The temptation is to spend ages formatting the page, choosing a font, and making sure that the font size and document zoom are all perfect, and this wastes time. It wastes those precious first few minutes you sit at the computer ready to write, and if your writing session starts slowly and is interrupted almost before it's begun, then you'll find it much harder to break through that and get on with the writing itself.

The next problem with word processors is that they will insist on formatting your writing, checking and commenting on the grammar as you write, and highlighting spelling mistakes in bright red wiggly lines, all of which is guaranteed to distract you.

So move away from the word processor, and try a much simpler, more basic solution instead. Notepad offers the writer everything you could possibly need, and removes those elements which could be distracting.

By using Notepad, or something just as simple, you can concentrate on the words, on the writing, and on the creativity. There will be time enough later, once the writing is done, to transfer it into a word processed document where you can format, edit and correct to your heart's content.

This tip aims to separate the writing from the formatting and editing, by separating the software used. If you don't use a computer, but have a tablet instead (such as an iPad) you can find a range of very simple text editors available which are ideal.

Tip #50

"Try using a pen and paper rather than a computer for a change."

The Idea

The problem with using a computer keyboard and a screen to write creatively is that you are physically distanced from your words. Your fingers keep leaving the keys, and the words appear on a screen some distance away from your hands. As you write, there's no physical, direct connection between your fingers and your words. This can sometimes be one reason why people experience writer's block.

Writing with a pen and paper is entirely different, and if you haven't tried this since school it may be worth giving it a go.

The great thing with writing using a pen is that your words are directly connected to the pen, which is directly connected to your hand, which is directly connected to your brain (effectively). There's no break, no separation, and this gives you more creative ownership over your words.

The process of writing is different too, because when you're typing you will be thinking one letter at a time, whereas with writing you will be blending one letter with the next to create whole words. With typing, your fingers disconnect from the keyboard after every letter, but your pen only lifts off the paper after every word.

The smooth process of writing can also help to keep the flow of thought going for longer, and you can even doodle in the margin, or leave notes for yourself - something which is much more spontaneous when using a pen and paper compared to using a computer.

It's surprising how many successful authors today still insist on using a pen and paper for their first draft, only typing it up after it's finished. You can have someone else type it up for you too if you prefer. Transcription or typing services are pretty affordable.

Tip #51

"Move away from the computer and make some notes or a mind map on a piece of paper."

The Idea

If you ever find yourself sitting in front of a computer staring blankly at a glaring white screen, the problem might actually be the fact that you're staring at a bright white screen. Try turning away, and using a more natural, more organic way of thinking.

Having a bright white screen in front of your face is a little like having an old desk lamp pointed at you in an interrogation room. The pressure is on, and every moment you're sitting there worrying about what to write the great white expanse, which seems to be getting brighter every minute, is reminding you in its own very stark, very blatant way that you haven't actually written anything yet.

If you've been sitting at the computer without writing for more than about thirty seconds or so, try turning away from it. Literally turn your back on the screen.

The break from the bright glare of the screen will help you to concentrate, and the physical act of turning away and seeing a different view can help you to vault over the wall that's blocking you from moving forwards, allowing you to visualise the scene, hear the conversation or understand the direction in which the plot needs to go.

If you find that simply turning away from the computer screen doesn't help you, have a notepad and a pencil behind you, and turn around to make a few notes.

Although what you write may be less important than the process of writing something at all, you may well find that when you're ready to turn back to your computer your mind is ready and willing to get the next words written down.

As well as writing notes, words or even a sketch, you may find that a mind map helps you to understand the bigger picture. Writer's block can sometimes be not because of the gigantic plot problems you're facing, but the niggly little details holding you back.

Mind maps are great for helping you gather these little details together into a more organised visual picture, freeing your mind to focus on just the points relative to the current passage.

Tip #52

"Draw a picture which represents what's about to happen next in your story or book."

The Idea

It honestly doesn't matter if your drawing is awful and embarrassing! No one is going to see it. The idea of this tip is to move away from the words. After all, writer's block is really all about getting the words down. Whoever heard of doodler's block?

Grab a piece of paper, and either draw a map, a plan of the room, or a fully realised landscape sketch of the location. By creating a visual interpretation of the scene you can look at things from a different angle, and notice things you may have not considered.

You may also find that using this method you can effectively storyboard the next few scenes of your story. In much the same way as a comic book has frames representing the action or dialogue within a scene, you can create rough doodles which do much the same thing. This conversion from words to visual images can help you to picture the scene much better.

Obviously it will take you a few moments to sketch even a rough idea of the scene and the characters, but these few minutes will give your brain, and in particular your subconscious, a chance to mull over the scene without being bogged down by words, sentences, grammar, spelling and punctuation.

Instead you allow your imagination to slip into a fully creative mode, which tends to leave behind the critical and analytical editor part of your brain which is primarily responsible for slowing you down, or grinding all writing to an unwelcome halt.

Don't be afraid to keep these sketches handy. Lock them away, by all means, and don't let anyone see them, but it may be helpful to occasionally glance at them, especially plans of rooms or houses, or even maps of locations, as they can be helpful reference guides later on.

Tip #53

"Reduce your writing session to just 15 minutes, 10 minutes, or even 5 minutes."

The Idea

You have organised your day so carefully, and now have a full hour ahead of you reserved exclusively for writing. So you spend the first five minutes making a cup of tea and organising a plate of biscuits. You then check email, and quickly update your Facebook page and Twitter feed. You take a glug of tea, nibble a biscuit, and begin opening the file you need for your writing.

An email pops up that simply has to be replied to, and then you remember you haven't checked your lottery ticket online yet. Tea's gone now, so you nip down to make another cup, and while the kettle's boiling you make a quick phone call.

By the time you've ended the call you've made and drunk your tea, so now it's time for another one. Then it's back to checking email again before you take another quick look at the file you opened. Presumably just in case the magic writing fairies have sneaked in whilst you were away and have written a few hundred words for you. They haven't.

If this sounds like you then one of the problems could well be the fact that you have allowed yourself such a long period of time for writing. All right, so an hour a day isn't very much, but for many people a whole sixty minutes of writing feels like so much that the procrastination excuses just rain down.

A possible solution to try is to reduce the writing time down massively.

By cutting it down to just ten minutes or so you remove the opportunity, and indeed the need, for delay tactics such as making tea and checking email.

If possible, pop a teabag in the mug, add a splash of milk and make sure the kettle's topped up - then leave it. Don't make it. You'll know it will be there ready for you as soon as you've done your writing session. Then make sure your email is closed down, and your web browser, and give it ten solid minutes of writing.

Tip #54

"Pretend you're phoning a friend, and start with the words, 'Guess what?' Then go on and tell the next bit of your story."

The Idea

We're all story tellers at heart, and especially over a large latte or a pint of best. If the phone rings and it's a friend we haven't spoken to for a while then we're bound to use the words 'guess what?' at some point in the conversation.

It's in our nature to want to share news, experiences and events, things we've overheard, or things we suspect about other people. This tip takes full advantage of that by getting you to role play this very common experience.

Now I know that to begin with this sort of technique might feel extremely weird, and you may feel rather silly. I do know however that a great many writers regularly talk to themselves, their characters, the wall, or even their cat.

Although the first time you try this you may feel a little self conscious, it's a technique you can practice and improve upon fairly quickly, to the point where you may even have a fictional friend you can talk to whenever your mind reaches a blank wall.

You can begin the 'conversation' by saying 'guess what..' and then recapping on something surprising or unexpected that's happened recently. If nothing has happened like that for a while in your story then you could start by saying, 'guess what I think is about to happen...'

Yes, it seems unlikely that something as obvious as this will work, but you'll be surprised.

Once we move away from being the typist, editor and proofreader and instead take on the role merely of storyteller our subconscious is freed from its usual shackles, and the imagination starts exploring various possibilities on the fly, and just one of those might well be the answer you were looking for.

Tip #55

"Increase the font size to something ridiculous like 50."

The Idea

You've been staring at the keyboard, hunting and pecking for at least half an hour, straining your cranial muscles and navigating through linguistic labyrinths, crafting what you believe to be a very passable first draft. You glance up, fully expecting to see at least a full page of text, only to realise you've managed about a paragraph and a half. No matter how good the writing is, there's a real temptation to feel disheartened by the lack of pagination.

Then of course there are those who will insist on asking you how many pages you've written today. To reply with a fraction isn't good.

And there's also the fact that you won't be able to merely glance up, establish the fact that the words really are appearing on the screen, and then glance back down again while you carry on. You will inevitably notice the spelling mistakes, and will begin re-reading what you've written.

This simple tip does away with so many of these daily problems. By massively increasing the font size you will find that these three problems fade away to the point where you don't feel quite so downhearted, and will be able to plough on with a more positive approach. Positivity is the enemy of writer's block.

By using a very large font size the number of pages, and the apparent amount of writing completed will look pleasingly large. Yes, you'll know it isn't truly representative of the actual amount, but it will take your mind away from analysing the actual length of writing completed. Once you exceed one page, you'll no longer feel that looming barrier.

The increased font size will also make it rather more difficult to quickly and easily proofread and edit your writing. You won't easily be able to see the beginning of each sentence, and so the temptation to edit will be much more easily resisted, allowing you to get on with the writing first.

Tip #56

"Buy a pack of tarot cards, shuffle them, and deal out four or five cards. Use the pictures as inspiration to make up, or continue, a story."

The Idea

Personally I don't believe that tarot cards offer any supernatural or psychic advantage, but that's not important. And that belief hasn't stopped me buying a few packs of tarot cards. I like them, and I like the way they can so easily be used to tell stories.

In fact this is very much the way in which people use tarot cards for fortune telling, simply attributing certain characteristics or symbolisms to each card, and then linking a randomly selected group of cards 'on the fly'.

Buy a pack of tarot cards, shuffle them up and deal out four or five. Do not worry about knowing the 'true' meanings of the cards. This technique almost works better if you're not familiar with them to be honest.

Simply look at each card, and attribute the first meaning or significance which pops into your head. There really is no right answer, and certainly no wrong answers with this.

You'll almost certainly find that it is fairly easy to see connections between each card in the sequence, and a story will often start to develop. It might not necessarily be a story you feel has enough merit to deserve being written down, but possibly something may come from it, and at the very least it will have helped kick-start the creative part of your brain.

But I often find that if I am stuck with a story, using tarot cards can often help prompt me to consider alternative ideas or options which I would almost certainly never have otherwise thought of or considered.

You can if you wish ask direct questions of the cards. Again, don't worry if you don't believe in any supernatural meaning - I certainly don't. But by asking a question about how your story can develop the cards will help you to access your subconscious, and often an answer or an idea will be forthcoming.

Tip #57

"Try free writing, preferably with a pen and paper to kick start your creativity."

The Idea

Free writing is a popular exercise in which you effectively bypass your conscious writing brain, and allow your wild, unrestrained and frequently bizarre subconscious to control your pen directly. To try free writing all you need is a pen or pencil, a pad of paper, a few minutes, and the willingness to write utter baloney!

To begin free writing, try to clear your mind completely, and then allow a word or phrase to pop into your mind. Don't question it, don't analyse it, just write it down. And then keep going. Just allow words or phrases to enter your mind without question, and without any apparent conscious effort.

Yes, you will frequently find that much of what you write is utter nonsense, making very little or no sense at all, with ideas and concepts haphazardly woven together in much the same way as a desperate drunk poet might do if he wasn't paying much attention, and had enjoyed a plate of somewhat dubious mushrooms a little earlier.

But the beauty of free writing is twofold. Firstly, it's a great way of accessing and unlocking your creative mind, helping you get into the right frame of mind for writing, and secondly, it can sometimes be extraordinarily surprising, revealing great ideas, hugely beneficial suggestions, and even entire stories, all seemingly from nowhere.

Now when it comes to free writing, and this particular tip, I do strongly recommend a pen and paper, or pencil and paper. This is because your subconscious mind is more directly connected with the words, and the fluidity of your writing will be improved. Using a computer is a little too forced, a little too distinct from the immediate creativity of your subconscious.

You can of course try free writing anywhere, and any time. Some people try it first thing in the morning when they have just woken up, others last thing at night.

You may want to try it just before you start your normal writing, but whenever you do try it, make sure you keep at it, as it's a skill and technique that improves with practice. And always keep your notes afterwards - you never know when a seed might start to form!

Tip #58

"Try sitting in a different chair. An ergonomic kneeling chair might be worth a go, or simply getting a pillow or cushion and placing it behind the small of your back."

The Idea

Ergonomics might sound like the sort of fancy thing thrown liberally into the conversations office furniture marketing reps might have, but the truth is that ergonomics often have a lot to do with writer's block.

If your body is strained or uncomfortable, your thoughts will be just as strained. Physical tension due to an uncomfortable chair or sitting position will almost certainly translate to mental tension, and this will in turn severely hamper your creative efforts.

Depending upon how long you spend in your chair at your writing desk you may find that you become more tense and more uncomfortable sooner or later, and this isn't going to help at all with your writing. Fortunately there are a few alternative solutions.

One solution is of course to buy a new chair, preferably one which has been ergonomically designed to be used for long periods of time. Although those large leather chairs with lots of padding look beautiful and feel comfortable, they are often described as 'manager's chairs', the idea being that they are designed to be used by managers who need to be comfortable whilst sitting back listening or chairing a meeting. They aren't as suitable for people who need to sit upright at a computer typing away for hours each day.

So when choosing an ergonomic chair make sure you go for one that has been designed for this use. Also, make sure it is fully adjustable so that you can sit on it with your feet flat on the ground, your elbows supported on arm rests that are the right height, and your back is properly supported for sitting upright.

Alternatively you may look at choosing one of those kneeling chairs which many people find useful. I have one myself, and it does make a real difference, helping to keep the back straight and reducing the amount of tension which builds up over time.

But you might also simply find that a change is as good as a rest, and having two or three different chairs available can help give your back, arms and neck a rest. Switching chairs can make you feel fresher. You might even simply stick a cushion under you, or behind your back.

I even sometimes find that it helps to stand up and write for a bit. I take a tablet computer with me into the kitchen sometimes and stand at the work surface writing!

Tip #59

"Re-read any reviews, feedback or positive comments you have received for previous writing you have done."

The Idea

Stephen King famously claimed to have wallpapered his writing room with rejection slips as a timely reminder of his previous journey.

Reminding yourself so frequently about the vast quantity of rejections you have had might work if you are a millionaire bestselling author, but for most of us such a constant reminder is likely to do more harm than good. We can be a sensitive lot, us writers.

Try to get in the habit of keeping a scrapbook somewhere of any positive reviews or comments you have received, from emails or letters to online reviews on sites such as Amazon. If it's a form of feedback, and it's positive, then it counts.

The important thing here is not to dwell on this collection. Spending too much time too frequently browsing through this collection of praise can easily result in you believing that this is the only form of feedback you have received. It probably won't be, and just as it isn't healthy to dwell too much on the negative reviews, it isn't wise to dwell too much on the positive ones either.

However, having those positive reviews somewhere can be beneficial should you find yourself struggling to focus on your writing, perhaps feeling dejected and unable to cope with the tasks ahead. This is likely to be at least partly as a result of your overly critical editorial brain trying to undermine your creative brain.

Having a scrapbook of positive affirmations of your ability to write is helpful, simply as a way of shutting up this critical editor we carry around in our heads much of the time.

By having a quick look through just a few of these positive comments you can reassure yourself that you are good, and capable, and that as long as you apply yourself well then you have the power within you to achieve good things.

Think of this scrapbook or folder as being like a sort of pat on the back you can give yourself from time to time.

However, as I said, please don't fall into the habit of looking at these positive reviews too often. A little self doubt is probably important since we all need to be reasonably self critical. But if you're struggling to get started, it could well help give you the boost you need.

Tip #60

"Write a dialogue between any two of your characters, using a dice to determine exactly how many words each will speak in their turn."

The Idea

Choose any two of your characters. They don't have to necessarily be from the same book or story, and even if they are, they don't have to be characters who normally interact. It helps if you have characters which are already established so that you can picture them fairly well.

Next, take a dice. This can either be a traditional 6-sided dice, or even an 8 or 12 diced dice. Decide which character is going to speak first, then roll the dice.

You must now write a line of dialogue for that character which is exactly equal to the number you just rolled with the dice. So if you rolled a 1 your dialogue might consist of 'Hello', 'Ouch!', or 'Damn.' It helps if you try to avoid the obvious words and be creative.

Next, roll the dice to see how many words your next character is going to speak. They must respond, in character, to whatever your first character said. In other words it must be a viable, believable conversation in which both characters remain true to their personalities.

With a 6-sided dice the conversations usually ended up pretty staccato, so you can always vary it by rolling two or three dice together and adding up the total.

This sort of false limitation exercise can be very useful, because your editor brain is distracted. Normally your editor brain leans over the shoulder of your creative brain, getting in the way and pointing out all of the errors and fallacies within our writing.

By using this sort of method to get a dialogue going two things happen. Firstly your editor brain becomes too distracted with analysing the numbers on the dice and checking up on you to make sure you're writing the correct number of words for each character to bother very much about the quality of your writing.

The second thing that tends to happen is that by throwing two random characters into a potentially unlikely situation you flesh them out a little, bringing them to life by viewing them from a different perspective. Since all good stories and books are essentially character driven, any exercise which helps to relieve writer's block at the same time as developing your existing characters is certainly a good thing.

Tip #61

"Write, 'It was a dark and stormy night', and then try to add an unexpected second clause."

The Idea

These words are of course from the famous (or perhaps infamous) opening line from Edward Bulwer-Lytton's 1830 novel 'Paul Clifford'. They are the most mocked, and most parodied opening lines ever written. You should never start a story with these lines.

Unless of course you're looking to have a little fun. Beating writer's block can be fun you know, and here's a case in point.

Write these opening words, which represent the first clause of the opening sentence, but then try your best to write the second clause in a way which is surprising, humorous, or shocking.

For example:

'It was a dark and stormy night, despite it being three in the afternoon and the middle of June.'

'It was a dark and stormy night when Edward Argyle realised he had clearly died several days ago.'

'It was a dark and stormy night that had lasted fourteen years, ever since the sun had been decommissioned to help combat global warming.'

This sort of writing prompt serves two purposes. In the first case it is likely to help you get your fingers hitting a few keys other than 'F', 'A', 'C', 'E', 'B', 'O', 'O' and 'K', and in the second it may well help prompt you to think about possible story ideas. Whether or not you keep the first clause is a matter for you to decide, but the second clause may well help kick start your creativity.

Being given such a bland first clause, and one which is so utterly notorious, is often just what's needed because your creativity has to rebel and react to this, coming up with something that's not just better, but is shockingly or surprisingly better.

You may be interested to know that this opening line has prompted an entire writing competition, which you can read more about here: http://www.bulwer-lytton.com.

Tip #62

"Use a random word generator to come up with 3-5 words, then use these in a sequence to tell a story."

The Idea

The human brain is astonishing at making connections, even when there really is no connection to make. This ability to make seemingly random connections between things is where déjà vu, coincidence and creativity come from. It's also where the benefit of this particular tip comes from.

There are several random word generators available online and these typically allow you to click a button or refresh the page to randomly generate a list of 3 to 5 words.

These words will be randomly chosen from a list or lists, and will have nothing to do with each other. Except that in your mind you will almost certainly see a connection. The challenge with this tip is to try to connect the three words together, in the order they appear in, to create a short story.

Sometimes you'll find the exercise fairly easy, sometimes you'll find the connections generate a humorous or downright bizarre sequence, and just occasionally you may find the seed of an idea glimmering at the back of your mind. There's nothing quite like the seed of an idea itching away like a grain of sand in an oyster to help give your writer's block a kick in the pants.

You can try this exercise in a number of ways. For example, you could limit yourself to just one sentence. For example, I just used my own random word generator at the page above to create a list which includes 'banana', 'bathroom' and 'pebble'. You might come up with a sentence along the lines of, "I was enjoying eating a banana whilst soaking in my bathroom when a small pebble with a note attached suddenly broke through the window above me."

Alternatively you could try to create a longer story, which includes a proper beginning, middle and end, and which includes the three randomly selected words. Whether you keep the words in the same order, or you're happy to use them in any order is entirely up to you. Set yourself the rules and then work to them to your best ability.

You can also use these random word generators to help you thrash out some new ideas within the constraints of your current story. So if you're finding your plot stuck, how would a banana, bathroom and pebble come into it?

For my own example of an online random word generator you can visit:

- http://www.justinarnold.co.uk/random.html

Tip #63

"Switch on your dictaphone and then try to get into one of your character's heads. Feel free to rant, complain, and ask questions of the author."

The Idea

Some people find it easier than others to talk to themselves, but if you can get over any initial awkwardness you might feel this sort of technique can be extremely effective.

If you don't have a dictaphone then you may find your mobile phone has a facility you can use for recording your voice, and if not then you may be able to use your computer. If you still have such a thing you may even dust off your tape recorder!

I find that the easiest way of getting started is to spend a minute thinking about which character I want to 'visit', and I make sure that there are no mirrors nearby. Catching sight of yourself talking in character is likely to be very off-putting!

Next I tend to look out of a window, so that the view doesn't include my own personal possessions and reminders of who I am. Instead I focus on trees, other people, the street, two cats scrapping - whatever happens to be on view at the time. Then I try to get into my mind, and start asking questions.

The first time you try this you may not find it terribly effective. That's fine, it is one of those tricks which gets more effective the more you do it. If the idea sounds appealing, then give it time. Practise it every now and then and you'll eventually find you can slip into character fairly easily. It's at these opportunities when sometimes you can really discover who they are, and why they are frustrated, angered, annoyed, upset or disappointed.

Good stories are character driven. If you're facing writer's block then the chances are high that the problem is character based. By diving into the mind of your characters and giving them the opportunity to vent their spleen you may find that the real problem is that your plot is not allowing your characters to do the things that they want to, or would naturally.

The moment your characters start dictating what happens in your story, the better your story will become. Many writers find that that moment is the most magical, when characters start taking the decisions, demanding that you merely write down what they say or do. Becoming a spectator of your own story is brilliant, and such times generally result in characters becoming more and more believable.

If you allow yourself to believe in your characters to the point where you can talk for them out loud, your characters are well on the way to helping you get over your block.

Tip #64

"Go for a walk with a dictaphone, and just record any ideas that come to you. Have it on auto record, and in a top pocket."

The Idea

Walking is a great way of beating writer's block - in fact almost any exercise is, especially exercise which is repetitive, and solo. Walking, jogging, cycling and running are all great. Scuba diving, volleyball and bull fighting probably aren't.

Gentle exercise helps to boost circulation, increasing oxygen to the brain, which helps you to think better. A repetitive motion or exercise such as walking or peddling a bike almost works as a form of meditation, the regular rhythm requiring minimal thought, but a reassuring regular beat.

Most people find that when they walk, run or cycle their minds start working through all manner of stories, plots and ideas, but it isn't always possible to remember them all. Stopping every few minutes to sit down and write in a notebook interrupts the regular walking, running or cycling, and this inhibits the flow of ideas.

This is where having a dictaphone in a top pocket, or at least somewhere where you can use it to record your voice hands free is ideal. I go running quite a lot, and have one of those arm bands you wear on your upper arm to keep your mobile phone handy. By slipping a dictaphone inside I can record my voice easily. When walking it easily drops into a shirt pocket or jacket pocket.

Experiment beforehand and see what works. Then when you're out and about you can just mumble away to yourself, asking questions, working through conversations, or just saying nothing until an idea or a questions pops into your head, and you can simply say it out loud.

Sometimes those little random thoughts which flash through your head when you're out on a country walk can easily be forgotten by the time you get back home. Having a dictaphone with you can be a real help. Many of your random thoughts may come to nothing, but you can bet that there will be at least one thing that you hadn't previously thought about, and that could be the key to moving things forwards.

I'm a great fan of dictaphones, because it is usually so much quicker and easier to make a quick recording than get a notebook out and start writing. It may feel a bit strange at first recording your voice, especially in a public place, but these days with hands free mobiles everywhere most people will simply assume you're on the phone anyway.

Tip #65

"Set deadlines and targets, and review them every morning and evening. Making promises to others helps too, such as writing groups."

The Idea

I know that writers and deadlines aren't a brilliant combination, and that if you want your writing complete by a certain date, don't tell the writer. But there are a couple of secrets to do with writing deadlines and targets which, if mastered, can go a very great way towards helping to solve any frequent writer's block which might be experienced.

The first secret to creating a target which you as a writer are likely to keep is to make sure that it is realistic. If necessary, lower your target, at least to begin with. If you would ideally like to see yourself writing a thousand words a day, then set your initial target at 250 words a day.

The chances are that if your target is easily achievable you'll be much more likely to achieve it. You'll also be much more likely to exceed it too, which means that you can feel good about exceeding your target, as well as knowing that you're making genuine progress with your book or story.

The other secret to targets and deadlines is to hold yourself to them by involving a third party. So for example you might simply tell your long suffering partner that your target each day is 250 words, or 500, or whatever you feel easily manageable, and arrange a time when you will report on your progress.

A better idea might be to involve a wider audience such as on Twitter or Facebook.

Get in the habit of posting an update at the same time every day, reporting how many words you have written that day. You'll find that people come to anticipate them, will comment on them, and you'll find yourself feeling increasingly obliged to update something reasonable each day.

Writing groups are another way of helping you tackle deadlines. If you're wanting to take along your manuscript for an appraisal or read you will need to have it ready. So make sure you volunteer to take it in at the next meeting, and then you'll have to hold yourself to account.

Also, make sure that at the beginning of each day, and at the end of each day, you review your targets and achievements.

Don't be tempted to transfer incomplete targets to the next day though - let each day speak for itself, not carry the previous day's debt.

Tip #66

"Build a house of cards Focussing on balancing the cards can help your subconscious focus on your plot difficulties."

The Idea

If you're at all familiar with Agatha Christie's detective Hercule Poirot you'll know that one of the methods he employs in helping to get his 'little grey cells' into gear is to sit calmly building a house of cards. It's a form of meditation in a sense, requiring calm, focussed concentration.

But how does calm, focussed concentration on something such as building card houses help with cracking the next stage of your plot? The answer is simply by giving your subconscious mind a bit of breathing space.

A writer's subconscious mind is where the vast majority of ideas come from, but all too often it is dominated by the conscious mind, analysing, fretting, obsessing and questioning. Often there's so much noise and bustle going on that the subconscious mind isn't given a proper chance do to its magic.

By focussing on an activity such as building a house of cards your conscious mind has to remain calm and focussed, which means that your subconscious mind can dust itself off and get to work. It is an unusual house of cards which doesn't result in a 'hallelujah moment' shortly afterwards.

Don't be fooled into thinking that this only works for fictional characters. Einstein was very good at building card houses too, up to fourteen storeys. His mind seemed to be in pretty good shape when it came to developing new ideas.

The trick to making this work is to think for a few moments first of all of what it is you need. Actually ask your subconscious mind to work something out for you. Be specific - place your order, and that's what you're more likely to get.

The subconscious mind really is a fantastic piece of machinery, because once you have specified your need, requirement or question, it will get to work - provided that your conscious mind isn't running around making lots of noise. That's where the activity of card house building comes in, keeping your conscious mind far too busy to hassle the subconscious mind.

Tip #67

"Always finish when you're on a roll, never when you're stuck."

The Idea

And no, by that I don't mean a bacon roll. If there's one thing guaranteed to make sure that your next writing session starts badly it's to finish your previous writing session at a low point, when you're stuck, out of ideas or feel drained of imagination.

On the other hand one thing that's very likely to help you get stuck into your writing straight away is to finish the previous session when you're feeling that the words are flowing freely, the ideas are coming to you and your writing is really moving forwards.

If you find that you can see very clearly where the conversation or action is going, and you have a pretty clear idea of how things will develop over the next few paragraphs or pages, then rather than keep writing, save the next section for the beginning of your next writing session. If you're worried about forgetting anything, you can make a couple of quick notes, but don't be tempted to do too much.

The slight 'worry' that you'll forget what's happening next is much more likely to manifest itself as a set of background thoughts in your subconscious. Your creative brain will be itching to get on with the writing and to get the thoughts down, which is a great way of approaching a writing session.

Knowing exactly what you're going to write next, or at least what's going to happen next, is ideal because you're much more likely to sit down and start writing immediately. The very idea of writer's block probably won't even occur to you because you'll just be so relieved to be getting your previous thoughts down.

But what you'll also tend to find is that by providing your subconscious mind with an unfinished section for it to dwell on a bit longer it will have developed ideas beyond your original thoughts. This means that as well as being able to get the thoughts down on paper from yesterday, you'll also have a clearer idea of the next section beyond that.

If this is the case then again, don't be tempted to get everything down. It is tempting to believe that your creative ideas are like songs on a breeze, easily blown away and lost forever. However, this is unlikely, especially if you have a regular writing routine.

This approach actually works well for almost anything, from exercise to painting. By finishing on a positive note your mind will be much more positive and open when you come back to it than if you finish by giving up and feeling frustrated.

Tip #68

"Try writing somewhere different, such as the library, a coffee shop or the park."

The Idea

Pardon the cliché, but a change really can be as good as a rest. Sometimes your usual writing surroundings can begin to feel so mundane, so ordinary, so familiar, that you can easily associate them with a sense of obligation, or of stress if you worry about your writing.

Getting away from wherever it is you normally hunker down to churn out a few more hundred words and plonking yourself in a fresh environment can do you the world of good.

Quite apart from increasing the possibility of you overhearing or witnessing something which might well make it into a future story, your mind is freed from the ordinary and the familiar, and this can make a real difference to your writing.

Last year I bought myself an iPad and installed an application which allows me to do basic word-processing without all the bells and whistles.

Quite often I have left the house and the familiar behind and have settled myself in all manner of new surroundings, from the local aquarium (The Deep in Hull - I recommend it) to the middle of a nature reserve, and from a local tea shop to a children's soft play centre (with my little boy - I don't go there alone!).

Strangely enough even though I'm the sort of person who, at home, has to have absolute silence to write, when I'm out and about it's the unfamiliar, new sounds which seem to foster a renewed sense of energy and creativity.

I know that if I head out of the house to do some writing I will easily complete two to three times the number of words compared to spending the same amount of time at home.

Of course, you don't have to buy a laptop or tablet, you could just as easily use pen and paper, typing it up later on. Try taking a notebook and pen out with you, with no other purpose in mind than finding somewhere new, and doing some writing. It can really be quite liberating!

If you work at home then you may also find that you're frequently disturbed either by family, or by the phone. By heading out for a couple of hours you can get away from both. Switch your phone off, or at least onto silent. You'll also find it easier to resist the temptation of doing some housework, or spending time on the internet!

Tip #69

"Make a cup of tea or coffee to get some caffeine through you, or a smoothie to boost your vitamins. In the evening you might even try a short of whiskey or similar to loosen your creativity."

The Idea

Now I'm not advocating chugging a gallon of coffee, nor getting blind drunk. Neither strategy is likely to see much in the way of quality creativity.

However, a little caffeine boost during the day, especially mid-morning or mid-afternoon can certainly help. Similarly, smoothies are fantastic for getting the brain firing on all cylinders.

It's easy to forget that the brain is basically a machine. Our creative ideas don't come from the ether. They don't drift on the air for magic fairies to catch and transfer into a mystical realm known as imagination.

Our brain is a soggy lump of jelly which is quite possibly the most complex thing in the known universe. And as it is fundamentally a machine, it needs fuel.

Fruit smoothies are a brilliant, quick, simple and easy way to give your body, and your brain, a real boost. The vitamins and energy in a fruit smoothie will really help give your brain the nutrients and fuel it needs to function well.

A good diet, along with plenty of fresh water, is really a fantastic way of helping to stifle any sense of writer's block. If you skipped breakfast or you haven't really had the most fantastic lunch then is it really any wonder that your brain is struggling to come up with amazing content?

I'm not going to turn this into a recipe book, and besides, there are shelves of smoothie recipe books at most bookstores, and vast swathes of similar territory online. A quick search on Google for 'fruit smoothie recipe' just now generated well over 10 million results, which should be more than enough to let you find a few you'll really like.

If you're writing during the evening then perhaps you might try to have a glass of wine or a glass of whatever your favourite tipple is. There aren't many jobs you can do whilst having a glass of plonk at the same time, but writing is one of them. Enjoy it.

Just remember, whatever you get down will never be the final draft anyway, you'll always edit it afterwards, so if you do hit a few wrong keys it really doesn't matter too much. Having a little drink may well help to quieten the noises being made by your editor brain, allowing you to relax a little and enjoy the journey your writing takes you on.

Tip #70

"Tell yourself that you are going to write 100 words, and then delete them so that no one will ever see them. Removing the pressure of potential permanence can help trigger a longer run of confidence."

The Idea

This tip may seem a little peculiar, but the idea is to try to overcome the fear or anxiety which can sometimes arise from a sense of permanence.

Being honest and realistic, nothing we writers write, at least first time round, is permanent. What we write will only ever be the first draft, and before it sees the light of day it's almost certainly going to have been redrafted, edited and reworded many times.

But sometimes it's easy to forget this, or overlook it, and feel that every word we write will eventually be used to judge us. That's where a sense of fear or anxiety can come from, and that fear or anxiety is the block which prevents the words being committed to paper or to the screen.

By stating to yourself that you will only write one hundred words, which isn't much, and that you'll be deleting those words once they're written so that no one will ever see them you'll gain a sense of liberation and stress free writing. Give yourself five minutes, one hundred words and a guilt free exploration of words, phrases and thoughts.

It's not quite free writing or stream-of-consciousness writing because it's more thought through, more structured, but it is still simply an experience of getting the first ideas and thoughts down without worrying about long term consequences.

Of course, like many tricks in this book this is a way of deftly fooling the subconscious and the editing half of our brain. The reality is that if you set yourself the task of writing only 100 words, and of deleting them afterwards, one of two things will probably happen.

Either you'll find yourself considerably exceeding the one hundred words, with the result that you simply continue with your writing as you hoped to do, or once you've written the words you don't feel you want to delete them after all because they're not that bad.

In either case you'll have cracked the block and have moved your story on, and that has to be a good thing. However, for this trick to work you mustn't expect or anticipate these positive outcomes, but simply enjoy them if and when they should happen.

Tip #71

"Switch the TV or radio on and listen to just a few seconds of speech. Switch it off and then write the words you feel they would have said next."

The Idea

As writers we tend to be good listeners. We tend to be the ones listening in to conversations, making mental notes, guessing what comes next, or picturing the person and their words at the other end of a telephone conversation to which we are party only to one end.

This tip taps into that skill. But it's important to do it correctly. Don't tune in to your favourite television show, or even to a programme you're familiar with. If you have the sort of TV package which streams hundreds of channels into your home then pick a number, any number, and tune randomly into any channel.

Then don't watch it. Yes, it may well be a television and they may well be talking about something you can't see, but that's fine. Deliberately shut your eyes or turn away, and just listen to the words. But don't do this for long. Just give it about thirty seconds, and then switch it off.

At this point you can do one of two things. You can either simply jot down the conversation as you imagine it might have continued, perhaps for the next minute or the next three exchanges.

Or you can make it much more interesting by imagining how the conversation might have continued had something dramatic suddenly happened. Such as an elephant wandering in to the studio, or one of the presenters suddenly proposing to the other, or accidentally dropping a suspicious package of 'herbs' from their pocket mid-interview. You get the idea. Such events in programmes more than likely would make them significantly more entertaining!

Of course TV and radio offer a fairly steady stream of dialogue, but they're not the only source of such dialogue. You can just as easily find yourself listening to snippets of conversation whilst nipping to the corner shop to grab some milk, standing in the queue at the supermarket or staring out of the window of the coffee shop.

Even standing in the playground waiting for your little darlings to emerge from school can present you with ample opportunities to listen in on snippets of conversation from which you can develop interesting ideas. Just make sure you get them written down. You never know when they might spark a possible idea.

Tip #72

"Begin by making a note of your target, and your reward, such as 'My target is to write 500 words, and when I have done that I will make a cup of tea'."

The Idea

The problem with a promise is that it's invariably not worth the paper it isn't printed on. A promise to yourself in your own head to write 500 words is so intangible that it is all too easy to ignore it, adapt it, edit it and forget it.

However, by writing that promise down, whether it's in type on the screen or ink on the page, you'll make it rather more tangible and real, and rather harder to ignore or edit.

If you are starting a fresh page on a fresh new day then get over your initial writer's block by writing your target and your reward. Straight away you have written a full sentence without any effort, and the page isn't looking quite as blank or intimidating any more.

Be realistic when it comes to creating your written targets. It's always better to overachieve than miss a target, because you'll feel so much better for exceeding your goal. That positivity and feeling of success can be a tremendous driving force, helping you to just keep going.

But also be fair and realistic when it comes to your rewards. It doesn't have to be anything fantastic or amazing. It could simply be ten minutes pottering in the garden, making a cup of tea or having a bath.

Try to avoid giving yourself rewards which can themselves be too distracting. Promising yourself that after you have written 500 words you will phone that old friend you keep meaning to, or go shopping for a new outfit will probably cause you to dwell on that too much, actually preventing you from getting the writing done. Small rewards work much better than big ones.

It's also best to keep your word count target fairly low, because there's a danger that you could end up focussing on the word count to the extent that you don't have your mind fully on the words themselves, and the story they're telling.

You know how much you are capable of writing in a single session, but I would suggest keeping the target low enough to be easily manageable, but high enough to be worthwhile. Generally this is going to be between 500 words and two thousand words.

Tip #73

"Try writing a sentence which includes no definite or indefinite articles."

The Idea

This is an exercise I suggested in my blog a couple of years ago, and it remains extremely popular. I very often receive emails or comments from readers submitting their own examples.

The reason why I originally suggested it was because of a somewhat bizarre writing job I was given by one of my clients. He required me to write an article, and then write three or four versions of it, such that any sentence from any article could be substituted with the sentence in the same position in any other article.

So the first sentence from article one could be followed by the second sentence from article four, then the third sentence from article two and the fourth article from article three. In this way he could create hundreds of variations of the same article.

The specific challenge though was that every version of every sentence had to be 100% unique. That sounds fairly easy, except that if I used the word 'the' in a sentence in one article, then none of the three or four alternative versions of that sentence could then contain the word 'the'. Similarly words such as 'a' and 'an' could only appear in one of the variations, and not in any of the others.

At first I found this incredibly tiresome and time consuming, but then after a while it seemed to become easier. I started to think differently during the writing process.

And then something truly astonishing happened. I actually found that this enforced restriction was actually causing me to be much more creative in my writing, and I very often ended up much preferring the versions of sentences which didn't contain any articles!

So try this. It may be challenging at first, but it's a fun little writing exercise, it certainly does get the brain cells warmed up, and it can be surprising just how your creative mind starts to make leaps and bounds.

I think one of the beauties of writing exercises such as this is that it demands so much of your creative brain's attention that your critical editor's brain doesn't stand a chance. For once those aggravating voices of doubt are silenced, allowing you to actually have fun with the writing process.

Tip #74

"Use Pinterest or some other image sharing site and find an image which captures your imagination. Describe what happens next, has just happened, or is happening out of sight."

The Idea

Be warned! This is one of those tips which can very easily be leapt upon by the subconscious imps which are responsible for procrastination.

Yes, it would be very easy to end up browsing board after board, page after page of interesting images, lurching from the simply imaginative through to adorable kittens, funny road signs and ending up with unfortunate screenshots of mistyped text messages. We've all been there, at least, if you're a writer, you'll have been there.

So approach this tip with a little caution. Done with a little self restraint it can be very helpful.

The best way of doing this I find is to limit the amount of time you're able to sit at the computer browsing images by doing something such as putting the kettle on to make a cup of tea. By sticking the kettle on and then sitting down at the computer I only have until the tea is brewed and ready before I have to start writing.

This means that on a really good day I may well find a suitable image well before the tea is ready, giving me a full minute or two to wander down an image strewn side road. Just don't let the tea get cold.

Once you have chosen your image, which can be anything from a mysterious deserted back alley to a castle half shrouded in mist, a densely packed wood at dawn or a busy city street corner, ask yourself one of three questions:

1. What has just happened that I have missed, arriving at the scene at this moment?

2. What is about to happen in a few moments at this location?

3. What is happening right now round that corner/behind that door, in those woods?

Feel free to start your snippet of writing part way through a scene or a story, making assumptions about characters which have already been introduced and developed.

Try also to be a little unpredictable, and avoid the obvious. Crimes down dark allies, kings in castles and fairies in woodland are all too obvious - challenge yourself to develop something unexpected.

Tip #75

"Allow yourself to use lazy writing, such as 'He stepped across the paper strewn room, his eye momentarily capturing [SOMETHING HAPPENING OUT OF THE WINDOW]', and fill in the blanks later."

The Idea

Sometimes writer's block isn't caused by the big things, but by the little things.

It might not be the mammoth plot arcs, the dynamic relationships between characters or the coordination of interwoven timelines that is causing the immediate problems. It might be as simple as how a character gets from 'A' to 'B', what the exact words were in a conversation which achieves 'C' or what the weather was like as character 'D' peered out of the window.

So leave these bits out.

Give yourself free reign to be lazy and take short cuts. After all, there isn't one single rule that says you can't, and if it helps you move forwards, then all the better.

So instead of spending another writing session mesmerised by the rhythmic blinking of the text cursor emphasising with every digital beat of its heart that your sentence still reads, 'Simone stared out of the window and watched....' transform it to 'Simone stared out of the window and watched [THE DREARY WEATHER AND RAIN AND STUFF].'

In fact there are two real benefits from doing this. In the first instance you'll find that by inserting a lazy shortcut like this you can move on from the place where you've been stranded and start to get on with the parts of the story that come afterwards, and which might be easier. So getting moving, making some progress is the first benefit.

But there's another advantage too, because if you happen to find yourself stuck later on in the story you can always go back through the book and pick out one of those shortcuts you included earlier on, and re-write that section.

By then you'll have got over the hurdle which existed at that time, you'll have developed the plot and the characters, and you may find that simply dipping your toe into an earlier section and filling the gap is easier, and makes a change from working in an entirely linear fashion.

Tip #76

"Do a 'Statler and Waldorf', going from one opinion to the opposite opinion in a single paragraph."

The Idea

In 1975 two characters joined Jim Henson's Muppet Show, Statler and Waldorf, two old men whose role was to heckle and criticise everything else on the show, and occasionally each other too. One of their most memorable arguments ran along these lines:

Waldorf:	That was wonderful!
Statler:	Bravo!
Waldorf:	I loved it
Statler:	It was great
Waldorf:	Well it was pretty good
Statler:	Well it wasn't bad
Waldorf:	Well there were parts of it that weren't good though
Statler:	It could have been a lot better
Waldorf:	I didn't really like it
Statler:	It was pretty terrible
Waldorf:	It was bad
Statler:	It was awful!
Waldorf:	Terrible!
Statler:	Terrible!
Waldorf:	Hey, boo!
Statler:	BOO!

I've tried this exercise with a number of people, where during the course of a single paragraph or short section of writing your opinion changes radically from one extreme to the opposite.

What you choose as the subject of the argument is of course entirely up to you, but try to choose something fairly specific, such as electric can openers. Here's an example:

> "If there is one single invention which marks humanity's progress it is the much underrated electric can opener. What other device could, at the mere touch of a thumb grant you access to food packaged in perhaps the most secure fashion, ensuring freshness and longevity.
>
> Whilst manual can openers may be a good deal cheaper, electric can openers provide the luxury of being used one-handed. Of course, the other hand invariably does nothing but wait until the can opener has finished its work, and naturally if the batteries are running low this can take a while.
>
> I do tend to find that if the batteries are going to run out, they'll do so at exactly the most critical moment, ensuring that your entire meal is ruined. To be honest, I much prefer manual can openers, and would highly recommend ditching the unnecessarily complex electric alternative."

Tip #77

"Write something which will get a more immediate response, such as a witty tweet or a blog post."

The Idea

One of the biggest challenges for a writer is waiting for a response. You can spend months writing a book, perhaps even years, and in all that time you are likely to receive little or no response at all.

Your cat, your partner and your mother don't count as far as opinions and responses are concerned by the way.

This lack of response to your writing can either make it all feel a little surreal, a little improbable or unrealistic, or it can lead to your self critical and highly cynical subconscious brain leaping out at you and casting gallons of doubt over your already troubled mind.

One way out of this situation is to gain a more immediate response to your writing. This can easily be as short, sweet and simple as a single tweet, or perhaps slightly longer such as a blog post.

The aim of this exercise of course is not to merely tweet what you have just had for lunch, or to write a blog post about how dull it is staring at a blank page for an entire afternoon.

The aim instead is to get a response. How do you do that?

There are various ways, including coming up with a witty or humorous observation, such as:

"Definition of writing: the process of spending as long as possible staring at a blank page or screen whilst contemplating household chores."

(@themightierpen)

Or it could be a blog post which offers help with an area of writing you feel confident about, such as title development, the avoidance of adjectives or how to understand the difference between who, whose and whom.

The idea is to try to elicit a response from your followers. This could include Likes, retweets, replies or favourites, but just getting that positive response can be a really helpful affirmation of your ability to connect to other people through your words.

I've sometimes hurled out a quick tweet such as the one above which then receives dozens of retweets and replies within minutes, and it can be a real boost. Of course, once boosted get on with your main writing as quickly as possible, knowing your potential audience is both real, and receptive.

Tip #78

"Try writing whilst standing up. If you have a laptop or a tablet, move it to the kitchen worktop and write there for a while."

The Idea

I have found this surprisingly effective, and for a few reasons. I think the most significant reason why this works is simply by shifting the body into a different position, relieving the stress and pressure on certain parts of the body, and improving circulation.

It's easy to forget that the body is simply a machine, and requires energy. The brain requires masses of energy, and that's only possible if the blood flow is good enough to get it there efficiently. By standing up and moving to a new location, and then remaining standing up for a few minutes it can help give a quick boost to the circulation.

I also think that this trick helps because simply by working in a different physical position, and physical space from the normal position and space you're familiar with you can find renewed focus and an ability to get on with the writing.

When you sit at the same desk and in the same chair, with the same view of the same few items every day it can become dull. It's also possible that those all too familiar experiences trigger memories or anxieties relating to writer's block, either real or imagined. By moving yourself away from the familiar, including the physical position and posture of your body, you can move away from those potential writer's block triggers.

Another reason why this works is that writing standing up doesn't feel natural. It isn't the way one would normally work, and it makes the entire experience feel somewhat temporary.

This feeling of only being there for a short while can help get rid of the anxiety that can be felt when you sit in your usual chair and know that your posterior is there for the next hour at least. Standing up in the kitchen makes you feel as though you're only going to be there for a couple of minutes, and that alone can make it easier to just rattle off a couple of sentences.

But what I have found is that I will move to the kitchen with my tablet, stick the kettle on, and then find that twenty minutes later I have written several pages, and forgotten all about both the kettle and the fact that I am standing up.

Tip #79

"Jump on a bus, any bus, going anywhere. Take a pen and paper with you and let your mind wander."

The Idea

If you're sitting at your desk struggling to let inspiration fall from the sky then you could be waiting an awful long time. Not least because there's a roof above your head stopping anything from the sky hitting you.

By getting outside, and getting away from the normal humdrum of your home study, kitchen table or office you can much more easily find inspiration strikes.

I think most people find it much easier to let their mind wander when they're on a journey, especially if they're not the ones driving. Buses are all over the place, and if you can spare a couple of pounds you can easily jump on a bus and find yourself zipping along, possibly through parts of town or countryside you don't normally visit.

If you tend to drive everywhere normally then getting on a bus can make even your normal driving routes seem different, since you are often much higher up, and able to look around you much more.

Make sure you take a notebook with you and a pen, and if possible try to leave your mobile phone at home. Escape, head off somewhere, with no destination in mind. You're not going anywhere, you're just moving, being driven down streets, across town, to the next town or through countryside, and when the bus reaches its destination you can simply hop on the next one heading the other way and come back again.

Whether it's the change of scenery, the gentle rumble of the engine and the wheels, the chance to observe new people in new situations or discover new buildings, alleys, secret places or new walks, or simply the fact that the scenery is rolling past you, changing every second, rather than remaining resolutely the same back at home, you'll find that it can be a real boost to your creativity.

What does tend to happen is that you can allow your mind to wander, to explore your story and to visualise ways forward. Make sure that you get those thoughts, phrases, ideas and images written down in your notebook so that once you get home you can get them written down properly, reinvigorated, revived and inspired.

Of course trains offer much the same, although they can be a little more expensive, and if you have access to a private jet.. well you clearly don't need much help achieving success!

Tip #80

"Switch keyboard occasionally, or use a different pen, or even a pencil."

The Idea

A change, so it is said, is as good as a rest, and sometimes it can be the smallest changes which do the trick. Like changing which keyboard you use, or even ditching your keyboard entirely.

Computer keyboards can be very expensive, but there are also some fairly cheap ones available too. Over the years I seem to have accrued about half a dozen different keyboards, and whilst I tend to default to a standard Microsoft Natural Ergonomic 4000 I sometimes find that changing the keyboard can make a difference. I'm not quite sure why, I just know that it does, and that it's something I would suggest trying if you can.

Of course, ditching the keyboard altogether is a more dramatic change, and that can make a big difference. If, like me, you have been using a computer keyboard for years, and use it for almost everything (including the weekly shopping list) then it's easy to forget the power of a pen.

The problem with a keyboard is that it disconnects you from your writing. Your fingers hit the keys on the keyboard, over and over again, and unless you pause to glance up at the screen you can feel that your writing is very remote, and distant from your imagination.

It's almost as though you're glancing at the screen and seeing something somebody else wrote. They don't always feel as though they're your words, that your brain and your fingers created. Replacing your keyboard for a pen and ink reconnects you with your words and your writing in a very real, and often helpful way.

When you're crafting each letter of each word with your own fingers your hand is actually touching the paper the words are appearing on. You can pick up the paper, hold it, and see the ink drying on it. You can't pick up your computer screen and feel that instant and direct connection at all.

The flow of the pen and ink, or even the pencil on the paper helps to encourage the flow of words and ideas. Keyboards tend to encourage a staccato of individual letters; pens and pencils encourage a flow of ideas.

Yes, you might not write as quickly, and yes, you'll need to type it up later, unless you use a transcription service, but if it helps you get through the next section of your book in a more productive way, then this is certainly worth trying.

Tip #81

"Go shopping without your wallet or purse, with the express purpose of listening in to snatches of conversation."

The Idea

I know the idea of going shopping without a wallet or purse sounds a little pointless, but once you've freed yourself from the obligation or temptation to buy something you can start to find that you're looking around you in a much more open and receptive way. You are allowed to take a notebook and pencil, but no money, and no cards!

Hearing snatches of conversation rather than entire conversations often gives you more to work on, because your brain starts to fill in the gaps. Listening to turns of phrase, questions, comments and ways of talking can be as helpful as the actual things people talk about.

Of course if you walk around a clothing shop you'll often find most of the conversations revolve around whether so and so would look good in this, whether anyone would be seen dead in that or whether the other would match their existing outfits.

But if you head into town and just mill about, or take a seat on a bench somewhere you can often hear snatches of conversation which fall like confetti, showering you in both the mundane and the intriguing.

Whilst listening to random bits of conversation you may well find that your brain is jogged into action and you find yourself moving your own stories on, perhaps with conversations which echo things you have recently heard.

If you're writing dialogue and you're finding it difficult then heading out to a public area and listening to people in ordinary everyday conversations can help stimulate you to then create conversations yourself which sound more natural and believable.

Having said which of course conversations in books are nothing like those we have in the real world. If you included every stutter, every pause, every um and er, every misunderstanding and random observation you would very quickly lose your readers. But sometimes it can become too stilted and unnatural, and this exercise can help you more easily strike the right balance.

On the other hand you might find that this sort of activity helps to give you ideas for other stories or scenes, and so it's worth getting these down so that if your writing brain starts to grind to a halt in the future you can always refer to these notes and work on one of those scenes or ideas for a while instead.

Tip #82

"Try changing the colour of the paper or screen you're using. Yellow is good."

The Idea

To be perfectly honest, black print on white paper or a white screen is a bad idea. It's just a shame that the default for most screens is black on white, and that most people write using black ink on white paper.

Anyone who is even mildly dyslexic will probably already know that it is highly recommended to either use slightly coloured paper and ink, or use a screen or paper filter, or even wear coloured glasses in order to make the text easier to read and understand.

But this applies to anyone, because after a while staring at sharp black print on bright white paper or a shining white screen is not good. The contrast can be tiring as the brain and eyes have to cope with such a very high contrast level, and this tiring can easily lead towards a state of mind which can be called writer's block. or at least writer-can't-be-bothered.

You might already be aware that in the legal world notepads are invariably yellow. You'll find most lawyers use yellow paper and write using blue ink, and this combination is much kinder on the eyes, and makes it much easier to focus on the writing, and understand it, without becoming tired.

The American Pad and Paper Company claims that the colour yellow was chosen for legal pads originally because it was more intellectually stimulating, but it certainly does offer less of a contrast. Of course, you can just as easily change the background of your wordprocessor to yellow, and the font to blue.

Although most people with dyslexia are very sensitive to the glare of black writing on a white background, either in print or on the screen, most of us tend to find this after a while to a certain degree.

It makes sense therefore to give the eyes and brain a rest, and change the colour of the paper you use, the colour of the ink you use, or the colours used in your wordprocessing program.

It doesn't have to be blue ink on yellow though, since there are various colour combinations people find useful.

Generally it is best to opt for pastel colours for the background, and then use ink or a coloured font which is below the very boldest, darkest colours. So if you opt for black, choose a darkish grey, and if you opt for blue, choose one which is not at the very brightest end of the blue spectrum, such as royal blue. However, feel free to experiment in order to find out what seems to suit your eyes and brain best.

Tip #83

"Take the first sentence from any well-known or favourite book, and use it to write a short (100-200 words) piece of flash fiction."

The Idea

Forgive me for pointing out the obvious, but flash fiction is often, at least at first, seen to be far less daunting than an 80,000 word novel.

I say at first because the challenge of trying to squeeze engaging and believable characters into a plot which is both realistic and entertaining into a space no larger than the summary on the back cover of a novel is not easy.

But knowing you only have to write a hundred or so words can make this exercise quite appealing. It's even more appealing when the first few words have been given to you.

It's an unassuming and unintimidating exercise, but one which will have the twin benefits of both getting your fingers to strike keys for a few minutes, or your pen to wiggle and wend its way across the page in the fashion common with those who not only refer to themselves as being writers, but actually go so far as to write.

You can either choose a book you know and love, a book you own because you feel it's socially expected for you to own it, or a book you've never read and know nothing about (feel free to nip to a bookshop and scribble down the first line or sentence from a random selection).

Once written down, try to abandon any expectations as to what the novel was supposed to be about, or who the characters were supposed to be, and instead let your idea run its own course. You only have a couple of hundred words, perhaps even just one hundred if you're feeling up to a challenge, so have a go.

Remember, simply getting your fingers typing or your hand writing is a huge step towards breaking the writer's block, and once you've started you can often feel it much easier to keep going. But you'll also find that with this sort of exercise you are perfectly likely to find the seed of an idea developing in your writer's brain.

Just occasionally you find a flash fiction story desperate to break free of its word count confines, and in such cases it may well be that you have the potential for a short story on your hands. But even if not, remember that there are plenty of flash fiction competitions available should you become fairly pleased with one such creation.

Tip #84

"End your writing session with a completely irrelevant question, such as 'why are penguins black and white?' Next time, begin by answering the question in any way you choose."

The Idea

You probably normally start each writing session either with a blank page, or with the most recent section of writing you completed. The problem is that unless you already have a brain brimming with ideas, or your last writing session ended at the point where you were desperate to keep going because you knew just how it would continue, you could be facing a type of block.

This trick tries to overcome that by presenting you with something that both links your last writing session with your current one, and also helps get your brain working.

By ending your writing session by writing a bizarre and absurd question, such as 'what would happen if a cloud suddenly fell to earth?', or 'what would it be like to live on the dark side of a planet on the edge of the universe and not realise there was a universe?' or even 'how would a penguin dress up for dinner?' you set in motion a number of things that can help you.

First of all, you end your writing session on something that's not directly connected to what you've just written, giving you an added bit of variety. Secondly, your subconscious is likely to ponder the question from time to time, and perhaps even give you an idea.

This means that you'll be thinking about what you will write the very second you sit down to begin your next writing session, which helps put you in a good frame of mind. You'll also find that by being able to write something creative at the very start of each writing session you'll find it easier to get on with the real writing afterwards.

Of course there's also the added benefit that every now and then you run the risk of coming up with an entertaining or interesting idea that might become the seed of another story.

Although dwelling on an irrelevant question and answer might seem counterproductive when planning and preparing for your next writing session, in fact it can have a very positive effect by distracting you from the problems or challenges of your book so that you approach it fresh each time.

Tip #85

"Use a wordprocessor which doesn't have toolbars, buttons or other distractions."

The Idea

The problem with most mainstream wordprocessors is that they are stuffed full of distractions. From scroll bars to menu bars, ribbons to buttons, status bar updates to zoom buttons and title bars they can be a nightmare for someone who just simply needs to type.

Fortunately if you find yourself too easily distracted by all of the buttons crowding in around your words, and even the distractions lurking outside the wordprocessor, such as the clock, task bar and so on, then what you may find useful is a plain, simple full screen text editor designed just for writers.

Fortunately there are several very good full screen, distraction free text editors around, many of which are completely free as well. I've used them, and I must say they are a boon.

It becomes so much easier to focus on the writing, and although checking your email, sending a tweet or updating your status are all just a couple of clicks away, because there's nothing on your screen except your writing it becomes easier to ignore the potential distractions lurking in the background.

Here are a few of the most popular distraction-free text editors available at the time of writing:

- **Q10** - http://www.baara.com/q10 *(free)*
- **OmmWriter** - http://www.ommwriter.com *(free version available)*
- **FocusWriter** - http://gottcode.org/focuswriter *(free)*
- **WriteRoom** - http://www.hogbaysoftware.com/products/writeroom *($4.99 on Apple's App Store or £9.99 to download for Mac OS)*
- **Writemonkey** - http://writemonkey.com *(requires a donation, which you can specify)*

I should note that whilst several of these are available for free I would encourage donations or upgrades to paid versions since often the authors of the software are writers themselves like you and me, and have created the product knowing the problems we all tend to face.

If you use one of these solutions to help keep you on track then consider it a little like buying the author a beer to say thanks!

Tip #86

"Ask yourself three questions your readers might ask at this stage."

The Idea

There is a slight danger here that you will be tempted to write three questions which you would like your readers to be asking at this stage, but that's not the point of this exercise.

Try to put yourself entirely in the shoes (or slippers) or your readers as they curl up with your book. Try to imagine what they might say if someone walked up to them and asked them to pose three questions about the book at that stage.

It could be that you imagine your readers might be asking why a particular character is always so grumpy and foul, or perhaps they might be asking whether the reference to a missing box is relevant, and worth remembering, or even whether the pace will pick up soon because there's been a heck of a lot of description or dialogue with very little actually happening.

Try to be critical and honest, try to remember that you are a reader yourself, and that you have often wondered about a book and its contents as you read through it.

Perhaps you have glanced ahead to find out how many more pages until the end of the chapter (is that perhaps because you don't want it to end, or you hope that it will pick up soon?) or you've gone back and re-read something because you weren't sure of a particular connection or relationship?

Try to ask yourself what criticisms or questions readers who don't know you might come up with at this particular point in the story. The chances are that your subconscious already knows, and suspects, that there might be a problem, and that could very well be what's holding you back.

By posing the questions yourself you can at least give yourself the opportunity of tackling the concern you have. if you think something might be distracting, get rid of it. If it's confusing, perhaps explain it more clearly, and if you think the pace is a little slow, move it along.

What you'll probably find is that if you are utterly honest with yourself and you both pose and answer the questions you think critical readers might be asking you can tackle the concern, and that in turn may well help relieve your subconscious from dwelling on your worries, allowing you to move on more freely.

Tip #87

"Try writing the next section of your text in an email. Compose an email to yourself, and write the text in the body of the email. Every 300 words, email it to yourself."

The Idea

Bear with me, this sounds bizarre, but it can work for some people. The principle here is that by changing the context of your writing you change the way in which your subconscious brain approaches the task of writing.

Think about it. How many times have you been struggling to write the next section of your book, with little success? And how many times have you struggled to write an email to someone? Probably far fewer times.

Of course it's entirely fair to point out that when you're writing an email it's usually for a very specific purpose, because you want to say a very specific thing, and it's only going to be a fairly short piece of writing.

But really, how is that different from the writing you're trying to do? If you're struggling to write 300 words of your book, that's really no bigger than a reasonably detailed email. And in the next section of your book are you not trying to say a specific thing for a specific purpose?

The point of course is that writing is writing, and it often doesn't matter what it is, who it's for or how long it is that really matters. 300 words is 300 words, whether it's a short story, a page of your book, a blog post or an email. Your writing always has a purpose too, since you rarely (hopefully) write fluff for the sake of fluff.

So try ditching your wordprocessor, and instead open up your email program or page, and begin composing an email to yourself. Insert your email address in the 'to' section, and then in the subject line you can write a summary of what the 300 words or so will be about. For example, *'Book: section in which Cara discovers the gate at the edge of the woods.'*

Then all you need is to start writing. Emails are far less scary than books, and if you're part way through your book you might find it fairly scary to notice the word count at the bottom. Emails rarely include this sort of information, and usually include far fewer distractions such as formatting and editing tools, buttons and menus too.

Tip #88

"Have separate sessions for writing, and for editing and proofreading."

The Idea

One of the biggest challenges for any writer is keeping the creative writing brain separate from the critical editing brain. Every writer has two 'characters', a little like the idea of having a small angel on one shoulder and a devil on the other.

Of course neither the creative nor the critical brain is either good or bad - they are both vital, but problems inevitably arise when they begin to conflict. As you are writing it is important to let your creative brain have free reign, to let it simply get the words down.

But this isn't easy if your editing brain is looking over your shoulder second guessing your choice of words, your phrasing, your plot development, your characterisation, your spelling, punctuation and grammar. The two are both essential, but should also be mutually exclusive.

Keeping these two apart is usually not easy for writers, unless they take the decision to keep them separate. The best way of achieving this is to designate some of your writing sessions to writing, and some to simply editing.

I know that some writers choose to spend the first section of each session editing, and the rest of the time writing, but I think that there is a danger in this for many people that the editing brain isn't going to shut up and go away just because it's been allowed to do its thing for a while. Keeping it out of your writing session entirely is often a better approach for most people.

It may be helpful to combine this approach with some of the other methods I have mentioned elsewhere in this book which help to keep your editing brain quiet, such as switching off any automated spellchecking feature of your wordprocessing software, and changing the contrast of the text and page colours so that you can only just see the writing, but not clearly enough to feel the need to re-read and edit it.

Editing is obviously of critical importance, and it is better to do this in a separate session where you can put your wildly creative brain to one side and approach your writing with a professional and judgemental eye.

Editing requires a critical and analytical eye, and this is as difficult to do properly with your creative brain itching to protect certain phrases as it is for your creative brain to enjoy getting something down with the editing brain leering over it the whole time. Separate the brains by separating the writing sessions.

Tip #89

"Choose a topic, and then write a list of ten words closely associated with that topic. Then write a paragraph about the topic without using any of the words on the list."

The Idea

This word exclusion exercise is easy enough to get started, but can offer enough of a challenge to make it interesting.

We all have ways of saying things, certain phrases or phrase structures, our linguistic quirks and individual idiosyncrasies. This sort of exercise forces us to abandon the tired old paths our sentences usually tread and instead try to create something different.

This forcing us away from our instinctive writing style can often help to get us excited about the process of creativity, and can be a good way of slipping deftly into writing what we actually need to.

Which topic you choose is entirely up to you. it could relate directly to whatever it is you're trying to write about, or you could choose something entirely at random. For example, let's choose the word 'lightbulb'.

The next thing to do is to choose the ten words which you think are most likely to be used when describing or talking about a lightbulb. These could include:

1. light
2. switch
3. bright
4. glass
5. switch

6. bright
7. lamp
8. filament
9. electric
10. replace

An optional rule you can include is to say that each of the words on the list also includes all word forms and variations, so that electric also includes electrical, electrically, electricity and so on. You now need to create a short piece of writing on the subject of lightbulbs without using any of the words on the list.

Choosing a word that relates to whatever it is you're writing about in your book or story can help prompt you to avoid clichés. The ten words above would almost certainly result in tired, dull and clichéd pieces of lightbulb related writing, but by avoiding them you are forced to be more creative, more original, and hopefully more engaging.

Tip #90

"Write a paragraph in which you kill off all your main characters in the most bizarre way possible."

The Idea

Who says that everything you write in your story or your book has to be sensible, or be ever seen by anyone other than you? By giving yourself permission to be utterly stupid with your writing you're taking back ownership of it, and rediscovering that it is something to have fun with, something to enjoy, something you have made and something you can destroy.

Killing your main characters is of course a little extreme, and isn't something that you're likely to want to include in any subsequent draft, but by writing something bizarre and ridiculous you will find that your editor brain takes a back seat.

Because your editor brain knows that this is ridiculous, and knows that it will never appear in any subsequent draft. It therefore doesn't bother to be overly critical, and this can allow your creative brain tremendous free will to be creative and mad.

It is of course highly likely that you will simply delete the section of writing at a later date, or even immediately after the session is over, but what you may find is that by creating the bizarre scene, by placing your characters in a situation that is far removed from anything else which takes place in the story, you are fleshing them out, getting to know them a little better.

After all, will you get to know what your character is truly like by watching them open and read a letter, or try to rescue a truckload of hamsters from a rampaging elephant that's escaped from the zoo?

Perhaps one of your characters arrives on the back of an ostrich, or a meteorite crash lands in the back garden. It could be that an army of ravenous zombies suddenly breaks into the town hall, or a deadly plague sweeps through the city giving everyone just four hours to live.

It's your world, your rules, but try to be as off the wall and unlikely as possible. Of course, if your story is already rather unlikely and off the wall you might find this difficult, but then perhaps if your story revolves around a meteorite storm that rains down on a zombie apocalypse you could introduce Queen Victoria to your main character, or reveal that his wife is actually a man. Go on, give yourself permission to have some fun!

Tip #91

"Have more than one writing project on the go, and switch from one to another to keep things fresh."

The Idea

Some writers tend to focus exclusively on one project at a time, writing nothing else but their book until it is finished, and then moving on to the next project after that. Others claim to have several projects on the go at any one time, but what they mean is that they are working on one project, and have notes on scraps of paper or scribbled in notebooks regarding other possible projects.

This suggestion is to actually write more than one story or book at a time. Perhaps have writing sessions divided into two, or alternate writing sessions, so that on one day you're working on project X, and the next day on project Y.

It is unlikely that if you have writer's block it will affect every project, and if you are struggling to develop one story idea or book then it may be easier for you to switch to another project for a while.

In this way you are more likely to keep things fresh, and you're actually using your writing sessions to write. As long as you're getting words down it may not matter whether they're for your book, or for a magazine article, or for a short story.

Of course it may be the case that you have a deadline looming, and I know from personal experience that a deadline looming large tends to encourage writer's block like nothing else. Usually it's the day before when I feel most inspired, and on the actual day of the deadline itself I feel as though there was never ever any real block at all, and wish I could go back in time to tell myself that.

But still, I do recommend having multiple projects on the go. How many is up to you, and of course it will also depend upon the level of detail and the length of the project. Having twelve full length novels on the go might be a tad ambitious, and you could find yourself very easily losing track of where you are.

But if you are writing a book then there's nothing to stop you writing a short story or two at the same time, and perhaps working on a magazine article.

What I do recommend is to mix your genres, or at least mix fiction and non-fiction together, So if you're writing a fictional novel, have a non-fiction work in progress at the same time. It's surprising how specific writer's block can be sometimes.

Tip #92

"Find a photo of someone who could represent your target audience. Print it out, and stick it somewhere in front of you. Talk to it and explain what you're going to write next."

The Idea

I've done something along these lines quite a lot, and it can really help. I think it's largely based on the fact that as writers we too often fail to have any clear idea of who our audience is. Putting a face to that audience, even if it's only representational, makes that audience seem more real, and helps us to relate to them better.

If you're writing a children's book for example, who are you writing it for? Just saying 'children' is no good, and neither is it terribly good to say 'children aged 5-7'. Unless you know quite a few children of that age well enough to picture them in your mind it's still a very abstract concept of audience, and this can make the whole writing process feel somewhat unreal.

So using your favourite search engine or image website find a picture or two of either an individual or a group of people who represent your audience. Print the picture out and stand it in front of your monitor, or nearby so you can see it clearly if you are writing longhand, and focus on that picture.

Imagine talking to that person, or those people, about your book or story, about what part you are on now, why it is important, and what is going to happen next. Explain to them why they will like it, and what they probably want to know about the story. Tell them what you are about to do, and why it is an important part of the book. And then get on with it.

Having a photo of someone who represents your audience allows you to create a more realistic dialogue with that audience that exists outside of the book or story itself. It helps you to understand in your own head what it is you are doing, and why, but from the perspective of your target audience, rather than merely because that's what you planned a while back.

I have a folder on my computer full of photos of various people, from business professionals to children, and depending upon what it is I am writing I will bring up an image and imagine a dialogue with that person, justifying what it is I am doing, explaining its significance, and explaining what it is I am going to do next.

It's a great way of helping to create an audience for someone who tends naturally to sit all alone in a quiet study for hours.

Tip #93

"Write out the final sentence from yesterday's writing session to start with. It may help you to slip back into the same train of thought."

The Idea

This is one of those simple tricks that sounds too silly and simple to work. And yet it does. Or at least it can. Like so many 'cures' for writer's block, or tricks that can help you break through it, it will work for some people for some of the time, but not everyone, and not for all of the time. It's another weapon in your writer's block armoury that you can bring out now and then.

When you become really involved in your writing you can find your mind blocking out whatever is around you, and you 'see' an entirely different world. You might be looking at a keyboard, a screen or a sheet of paper, but what you're actually seeing is that other world you're writing about.

By writing out the last sentence of your previous writing session there's a chance that you can get back into that same frame of mind, and step into that other world as though you never took a break at all.

What I would not suggest doing is staring at the words you write for the previous sentence and copying them down exactly, because all your focus is going to be on the words, and not the meaning or the visual ideas they represent.

Instead simply re-read the last paragraph of your writing, and then choose a point that's a line or two from the end. Make a rough mental note of what the last couple of lines achieved, explained or said, and then without looking at them, and without trying to get them absolutely accurate, write them out.

I suggest inserting a page break, creating a new document or starting on a new sheet of paper so that you're not distracted by the exact words you used last time. Instead simply try to get the general message across.

The less you focus on getting the exact words right, the more you are able to focus on the meaning, the tone and the message, and this is what is more likely to help you get back into that world, and to occupy the virtual head you were seeing that world through last time.

Of course you may find later that your second version of the two lines you wrote out is better than the original ones, but don't worry about trying to achieve this deliberately.

Tip #94

"Write a conversation between two of your characters, no matter how mundane it might be."

The Idea

I've said it before, but it's a hugely important message - great stories rely massively on great characters, and great characters are believable.

If you're struggling with a story then it is probable that you are focussing too much on elements which are not character led, or your characters are becoming too flat, too one dimensional, or are acting in a way which doesn't reflect how they probably would act if they had free will.

The idea behind this tip therefore is to help develop your characters, but in a way which doesn't involve you having to use them in your story or book itself.

By doing an entirely separate piece of writing which involves those same characters, but knowing that no one will ever read that section, you can have fun exploring your characters' traits, habits and way of speaking in a way that can then translate to you being able to use them more effectively and more naturally in the story itself.

You can take a character from your book which you are currently using in a scene, and you can combine them with any other character from your story. It doesn't have to be a character who is involved in the same scene from your book, it can be any character, even one they would never normally meet in your story. You can choose major characters or fairly minor ones who might normally have barely any dialogue at all.

The point is that you need to set up a situation in which those two characters are interacting and engaging through dialogue, in a situation that may be pretty mundane.

It's often in fairly mundane situations that people's idiosyncrasies become apparent, perhaps choosing from a menu, engaging in small talk in a lift or sorting out insurance details after a prang.

Of course you could include additional characters, but I would tend to keep it fairly simple so that you are able to focus on the main character who may be causing you difficulties.

Having written your 'off the record' dialogue you may find that in your mind they have stepped out of the shadows and become a little more real and a little more believable, allowing you to use them to help you move your story forwards.

Tip #95

"Make a request for inspiration about something specific just before you go to sleep, and make sure you keep a pad and a pen by the bed."

The Idea

The subconscious is an amazing thing, and it works in ways which we barely even begin to understand. Why it is that 48 hours after failing to remember someone's name it will suddenly leap into your mind whilst you're thinking about a new recipe for dinner is testament to the fact that it's often working busily away in the background without you even being aware of it.

Your subconscious is thinking about different things to you, almost as if it's an entirely separate mind.

If you're struggling with your book or your story and you feel you need help then enlist the support of your subconscious mind. It's enormously creative, and very hardworking - it even works while you sleep, and this is the key to this tip.

Right before you are ready to go to sleep ask your subconscious mind a question. It's best to be fairly specific. Questions such as 'I need an idea for a new best-selling book please' might not work, but you could try things such as 'what would this character do in this situation?', or 'how can I show how this character feels discovering the letter?' or 'what is going to happen next?'

There's no guarantee that you'll wake up with the answer, and even if you do get an answer there's no guarantee that it will be the very next morning. It could wake you up at three in the morning, or it might hit you with the answer two or three days later. It might not come at all, but it's surprising just how many times it does work.

Of course, there is always the risk that your subconscious mind will give you a solution which you feel is in complete contradiction to the story so far or to the situation your characters are in, or even how they have been behaving. But take notice of the messages you've been given nonetheless, because they may be telling you something you don't want to hear.

If you feel your subconscious is showing you a way for your characters to behave which doesn't fit with how they have been behaving so far, then it could be that you have not been allowing your characters to develop fully and naturally, and by letting them change you create more believable characters which in turn allow you to create a better story.

Tip #96

"Take a section of your writing that's purely descriptive, and turn it into dialogue instead."

The Idea

You have probably heard of the advice to writers to 'show, not tell', and this tip very much encourages this sort of approach. Basically you don't need to tell your writers that character X is angry, because you can demonstrate this by describing his angry behaviour, and the way he looks. Showing someone being angry is much more engaging than merely labelling them.

One of the easiest ways of showing readers what's happening rather than merely telling them is to get your characters to do the talking for you. Obviously this doesn't mean that character Y simply says that character X is angry, they can show this through their words in a much more effective way.

I've said before, as have many others, that good stories are almost always character led, and that if you can create strong, believable and interesting characters your story is almost written. Dialogue helps to show your readers not only what is going on, but also shows them what your characters are like.

Long passages of description might be fun to write, especially if you enjoy showing off your creative metaphors, but they don't help to flesh out your characters, and without characters your plot isn't going to move very fast. In fact it's highly probable that your plot wouldn't even get started unless your characters got up and did something.

Select a part of your story where there is a fair bit of description, especially if there hasn't been much dialogue for a while, and try re-writing it as dialogue, or at least largely as dialogue.

Whether you end up using this passage is up to you. I would suggest including it in your manuscript for now, as an alternative section, and you can decide later which version you're going to keep. But as a writer it's a good exercise even if you don't end up including it because it helps you to flesh out your characters in your own mind, get into their heads a little better, and make them easier to write in future.

If you don't have a good opportunity to get characters to talk, because perhaps there's no one around, then get them to talk on the phone with someone, to their pet cat, to their god, or even to their reflection in a mirror.

Tip #97

"Create a routine. Set a time to sit down and write, with a time limit or a word count limit (say 500 words)."

The Idea

Some writers like to wait until inspiration strikes like a bolt from the sky before hitting the keyboard or wiggling their pen. Other writers just write, and it should be no surprise that of the two types of writer the one most likely to succeed is of course the latter.

Wannabe writers wait for inspiration; real writers just get on with it. Because the truth is that inspiration is fickle, and you could be waiting hours, days, weeks or even years for that bright idea. In the meantime your word count is looking decidedly bleak, your keyboard decidedly clean and your pen decidedly ink-laden.

Rather than waiting for inspiration, create a routine, such as writing for half an hour every day starting at 6.30 am sharp, or 9 pm on the dot, or whenever suits you. Create a routine, and stick to it. Even if you don't feel inspired, get your posterior on the chair, and write.

Remember that your first draft is only your first draft. No one expects the first draft of even the most celebrated author to be very impressive. The first draft is the skeleton of your book, nothing more. In fact it's barely even the skeleton, because you'll probably add a few bones, toss out a few others and change the order and structure way before adding flesh.

If you create a regular routine then it's surprising just how well your subconscious tends to twig this, and get you some ideas ready. But even if you find you're staring at a blank sheet of paper or a blank screen, get something down. It doesn't matter how rubbish, it's only a first draft, no one will ever see it.

It's important to set yourself a regular routine for many reasons, not the least of which is to give your writing 'muscles' their regular exercise. Yes, I know people talk glibly about writing muscles, and I know it's only a metaphor and therefore not to be taken literally. But it is certainly true that the more you write, and the more regularly you write, the easier it is to write.

Routine is important because it prevents you from allowing too much time to slip by whilst you wait for your inspiration. Remember, you're just a writer, the world doesn't owe you inspiration. Sometimes you have to get by with simply making something up.

Tip #98

"Imagine you are one of your characters taking over the writing process for you."

The Idea

How well do you know your characters? How well would you trust them with your writing? This idea seems a little bizarre, and whilst it won't work for everyone, and certainly not all the time, it's one of those many little tips which can work occasionally, and is well worth bearing in mind. So how does it work?

Whether you try this tip out with your main writing, or with a separate piece of writing that's not intended for publication at any stage is up to you. If you're concerned that the writing style would simply not fit if you tried writing in a character's voice then remember that you're almost certainly still only on a first draft. To a certain degree it doesn't really matter if the voice isn't quite right. Having the bones of your story written down rather than floating like wisps through your mind is the first and most important step.

Try to picture a character from your writing as clearly as you possibly can in your mind. Importantly, try to hear their voice.

Picture them talking, and hear their style of talking. Picture their mannerisms, the way they emphasise certain words, the way they explain things, the way they pause occasionally to gather their thoughts, perhaps the sound of their voice. It really helps to picture your character not as a puppet, but as the puppeteer. Give them life, give them a personality and give them a voice which you can't just read, but can actually hear.

Then get them to write. Or at least, dictate. Hearing them explain what's happening will give it a slightly different slant, but if you think of it as dictation rather than dialogue, or monologue, then you'll find it easier.

Of course, the main benefit of this is to simply get words down, and to flesh out a character a bit more while you do it. If you want to throw the end result away, or edit it to the last full stop, that's up to you. But you might also find that you can use the piece in some way - even as a diary entry or similar.

Even if you don't think there's any way in which you can include the piece in your final copy, you will find that your character will have made observations, or expressed opinions or suspicions that perhaps you hadn't really considered much yourself, or indeed at all, and these could help nudge your own writing on a little.

This sort of exercise also helps to invest more life and background into your characters, which in turn often has the effect of making the writing process easier.

Tip #99

"Change the font to Windings, or something else that's more pictorial than alphabetic."

The Idea

Why on earth should this help at all? It sounds like a really stupid idea. After all, what publisher or agent would want to spend more than a blink of an eye looking over a manuscript which looks as though it's written in hieroglyphics or something? Well, there is definite method in this apparent madness.

If you've read a few of the tips and tricks in this book, or even read through the whole of it up to this point, then you'll be aware of the fact that as a writer you have two brains: the writing brain, and the editing brain.

It's almost impossible for writers to switch off the editing brain while they write, especially on a computer. With every word, with every line, the editing brain is quickly scanning for spelling errors, formatting issues, grammar mistakes and other potential problems, a task made easier by the fact that most wordprocessors by default underline or highlight spelling mistakes and grammar mistakes.

This editing brain really gets in the way of the creative writing brain, and during the creation of the first draft this isn't helpful at all. Editing is essential of course, but there is a time for that, and it's after the first draft has been written.

So what does this all have to do with writing your first draft, or some of it at least, in an entirely meaningless font such as Windings?

The answer is simple - by using a font you can't read, your editing brain can't edit. You can glance at the screen, but since you have no idea what the symbols mean, you can't be tempted to analyse it, look for spelling mistakes or other problems.

In this way your editing brain will eventually just give up and leave your creative brain to it. At least that's the theory. I find it does work sometimes, and I know it has worked for many other writers, and so it's definitely worth a try.

Interestingly one thing you may find is that even though your writing appears to make no sense, spelling errors and potential grammar errors will continue to be highlighted by the software. However, since you can't correct those mistakes, or even identify them, your editing brain should be happy to wait quietly until your creative brain is done. Then simply highlight the text and switch the font back when you're ready to edit.

Tip #100

"Go back and re-read something you wrote a while back that you are really proud of, and remind yourself that you are that writer."

The Idea

As writers it is very easy for us to become caught up in the here and now, to obsess not simply over the book we're currently writing, and not even the chapter, but over each line, each word. With each clause we criticise ourselves, pouring doubt on what we suspect may be self delusion.

It is easy for us to forget our successes, by which I don't necessarily mean those books, articles, stories or poems which have been published. Publication doesn't necessarily denote success in terms of writing style, or even writing quality. Publication merely means that someone believes they can make money from something you wrote.

If you're stranded midway through a book or a story and your own personal demons are trying their best to drag your spirit down and pour scorn over your efforts to string a sentence together, despite it being something which almost every other human being manages hundreds of times a day without barely a thought, then try this.

Somewhere, either published or unpublished, there will be something you're proud of. Something special, something that seemed to come from somewhere beyond the confines of the five pounds of jelly squished into your skull. Go and find it, sit down with it, take a moment and read it. Remind yourself just how good you are, and that those words were written by you. Remind yourself that you are a writer, that you have written, and that you have written words that actually make you feel proud.

If you have received reviews for your writing, such as book reviews, or even letters or emails from clients who were particularly pleased with your writing, then read those.

It sometimes seems that the definition of a writer is someone who has less faith in their ability to write than a normal human being. Perhaps this is so, but that's really only because we invest so much energy into subtle nuances, unique expressions, finding ways to paint a picture and evoke a feeling using just a scattering of squiggles on a page.

It's something you've done before, and whilst not everything we have ever written is remarkable or something of which we can feel especially proud, there's bound to be something. You probably know what it is. Don't hide it, don't avoid it, remind yourself what you can do, and re-discover the feelings of pride that writing evoked in you before, and let it inspire you to have faith that the words will flow again.

Tip #101

"Reduce your daily writing target to just 50 words. Next time make it 100, then keep increasing it incrementally, keeping to the limit no matter how tempting. After a few days you'll be desperate to just keep going."

The Idea

Do you feel your writer's block is partly because of the mammoth task ahead? Would you expect to face the same sort of difficulty if you were about to write a shopping list? A short email? A memo?

By reducing the word count target from several hundred or even thousand words to a much more manageable level you are effectively reducing the size of the task ahead, and therefore the anxiety which comes with that. Writer's block is mostly a result of anxiety, and so the first step to resolving the situation is to lessen or eliminate this anxiety.

Fifty words is nothing. Fifty words is about two lines of writing on this page. It's barely a couple of sentences. It's certainly nothing to become unduly concerned about.

So instead of sitting down with an hour, three hours or six hours of empty writing time ahead of you, set your target for today at just 50 words. Be honest, and make every word count, but stop at fifty.

Tomorrow, increase that word count, perhaps by another 50, so that you're stopping at 100 words. The next day, increase it again by 50, and keep doing this for a week. After seven days your daily target will be 350 words, at which rate an 80,000 word novel would be written in 228 days, or around seven and a half months.

Of course this might be realistic, but it's not going to get you throwing a handful of novels at your publisher or agent each year. If you're wanting to be more productive then clearly you need to increase that word count still more - but how?

In fact you'll probably find that after seven days of incrementally adding 50 words to your daily target you won't even need to ask that question.

Because by sitting down for seven days and meeting your daily target every day not only will you already start to feel you're making progress, but you'll probably find that you're itching to write much more than 350 words anyway, and will have forgotten you ever had a block.

Tip #102

"Do not open up your web browser or email program. If they're open, they'll be there to tempt you. Have a timetable for when you will open them, and afterwards make sure you close them again."

The Idea

How do you know if you're truly a writer? The answer could very well be that you spend an inordinate amount of time avoiding doing any writing. It is highly probable that if you use a computer of one kind or another to do your writing you'll find both your email and your web browser get far more attention than any novel you're working on.

Certainly whenever I make a comment through a social media platform such as Twitter where I can reach many thousands of writers and authors it is invariably those observations I make regarding procrastination and the misuse of online distractions to avoid writing which elicit the most number of responses and actions. In other words, if this sounds like you, you're in extremely good company.

But being in good company doesn't necessarily help with actually getting any writing done. The answer can sometimes be surprisingly simple. If you use an email program rather than accessing email through your browser then it's quite possible that one of the first tasks in the morning is to open it up, and one of the last at night is to shut it down.

It might be worth getting in the habit of only opening the email program once every now and then, perhaps before your writing session and afterwards. After all, what sort of emergency situation would require you to access an email instantly anyway?

The same is true with your web browser. If it's open then it is barely a single click to switch windows and start browsing. Perhaps you have a number of tabs open already, and so it only takes a couple of clicks to be browsing the news, checking out the latest videos and seeing what everyone is up to on Facebook. So close it.

Right before you writing session, just close your browser. Close everything in fact, except for your writing package.

Okay, yes, it's perfectly true that you could easily open those programs again with a single click, but having them closed does two things. Firstly it puts you in mind for writing, knowing that you have to take deliberate action to avoid writing rather than merely 'glancing' at something already open, and secondly, you won't be distracted by popup alerts or beeps which indicate you have new mail, or messages.

Tip #103

"Break the rule about adverbs - write dialogue which includes as many as possible."

The Idea

It often strikes me as ironic that in schools children are taught from an early age what adverbs are, and given exercises which encourage their use, yet when learning to write professionally one of the first lessons is how to eliminate adverbs as much as possible.

If the idea of not using adverbs is a new one for you, then basically it stems from the 'show don't tell' rule of writing. In other words, don't tell me that the character is angry, show me what they are doing and saying, and I will work out the fact that they are angry for myself, and enjoy creating that impression for myself much more.

You can often spot an amateur writer as they tend to include a huge number of adverbs, those words which often end in '-ly', such as happily, sadly, blindly and hurriedly. An adverb describes a verb or action. How did she run, how did she cry, how did she shout, how did she congratulate?

It's easy to say 'she congratulated him happily', but rather than tell me 'this character is happy' show me this by describing what she is doing. if she is smiling, laughing, jumping up and down and clapping him on the back, then I can pretty much work out that she must be happy for myself, which makes for a more satisfying read with characters more likely to have depth.

But for this tip this rule goes out of the window. Instead of trying to avoid including adverbs in your writing, try to add as many as you can.

"You're mad," she muttered quietly.

"No my dear, I can assure you I am perfectly sane," he replied menacingly.

"It was you all along, wasn't it?" she exclaimed desperately.

And so on. You get the idea. Appalling, quite appalling, but trust me there is reason in this madness. By including as many adverbs as you can two things will happen: firstly, you'll have a bit of fun, and secondly, your annoying editor brain will take a back seat, knowing your writing isn't serious.

But then comes the clever part - because when it comes to the redraft, take every adverb delete it, and replace it with action which reveals the intent behind the adverb in a far more professional way.

Tip #104

"Use Lego to build a set for your story, and 'play act' the scene."

The Idea

Firstly let me make it perfectly clear - you are never too old to play with Lego. Once you have that fact firmly understood we can move on. Of course whether you use Lego or another similar sort of building block is entirely up to you, but what's important is that this will help you to become engaged with your writing again. Let me explain.

Visualise the scene just before the point at which you're stuck in your story. Now tip out a large box of Lego bricks and build a rough approximation of the scene and the characters. Don't for goodness' sake go too crazy about the accuracy of anything. That way procrastination doth lie. Instead just have a bit of fun mocking up a sort of stage set that works well enough.

Now some people will be able to do this very easily, and others will feel too self conscious. I would guess that if you've read the tip at the top of this page and read down this far that you're probably in the first camp and understand entirely what I'm getting at. If you don't feel you could sit down with a box of Lego and just play then I feel very sorry for you. You're missing out!

Part of the benefit however is in the actual construction of the set. Just by working in a kinaesthetic way you start to create a real version of your fantasy world, and create a hands on connection to that world. Even if you don't play with the characters in that set, you will find that through the building stage you will start to imagine your characters interacting and engaging with both the world and each other, and this could well be the catalyst you need for moving things forward.

However, if you do have the lack of inhibition required to play with your bricks then simply act out a rough approximation of the recent events in the story. Feel free to speak out loud for your characters, but an internal dialogue is perfectly fine.

Yes, it may well feel funny at first, and you will probably want to shut the curtains and make sure that everything is tidied away afterwards before anyone sees you. But if you have never tried this sort of thing then you'll never know how really helpful it can be.

Obviously there is a danger that you could end up using this sort of exercise as a distraction, but I personally believe that if you have the ability to absorb yourself entirely in a world made of small plastic blocks, then you have the imagination and creativity to create absorbing worlds and characters made entirely of ink.

Tip #105

"Write one sentence which consists of exactly 70 words, and then one sentence to follow on from that which consists of just 7 words, with the two sentences forming one complete paragraph."

The Idea

This is an interesting, and often very effective technique to use. It's important in writing to make sure that you try to vary sentence length. if every sentence is pretty much the same length then the pace can feel somewhat lacklustre. By changing the length of sentences occasionally you can change the rhythm and make the words stand out that bit more.

In this exercise there are a number of challenges, the end result often being that you end up with a paragraph that's pretty good for a first draft, and often helps you to continue the writing from that point.

One of the most difficult aspects of this exercise is writing a sentence that's 70 words long which doesn't sound too longwinded or deliberately drawn out. You aren't allowed to use semicolons or colons, but you can use commas. The first sentence must be exactly 70 words in length.

You then have an extremely sharp change in pace with the second sentence being just 7 words long. This creates a contrast which can be extremely effective. Have a look at this example to get the idea:

"*Tumbling head over heels hurtling down the hill Sara caught flashes of trees, glimpses of rocks and a kaleidoscope of flashes interchanging sky and ground, her legs cracking on the frozen surface as white clouds and white snow became a tangled blur, the only constant being the seemingly never ending rush of wind as she fell further and further, the distant cries of her family becoming lost amongst the confusion. This is it, she thought, I'm dead.*"

Whilst I certainly wouldn't recommend including this sort of contrast in sentence length very often, occasionally something like this can really perk up the pace. As well as being a useful writing exercise it's also a reminder to think about sentence length and pace.

By focussing on a single sentence in this way, trying to create a lengthy but engaging 70 word sentence, you will probably find that by the end of it you'll be ready to simply keep going.

Thank you!

Thank you for buying and reading this book. I hope you have enjoyed reading the suggestions, and have found some of them to be really useful to you with your writing.

I would love to hear from you about your experiences with trying out some of these techniques, especially where you have found success.

You can connect with me on Twitter (@themightierpen), through my **copywriting website** (http://www.themightierpen.co.uk), through my **author website** (http://www.justinarnold.co.uk) or directly by email, me@justinarnold.co.uk.

For further information, advice and support on writing and on the English language you may be interested in following either (or both) of my blogs, which you can find at:

- http://www.themightierpen.co.uk/blog
- http://justinarnold.co.uk/blog

Share your favourite tips and recommendations on Twitter using hashtag: #105ways

Printed in Great Britain
by Amazon

44687025R00127